YAOMING

Read all of the books in this exciting,
action-packed biography series!

Alex Rodriguez

Annika Sorenstam

Barry Bonds

Cal Ripken Jr.

David Beckham

Derek Jeter

Doug Flutie

Eli Manning

Hank Aaron

Ichiro Suzuki

Jesse Owens

Jim Thorpe

Joe DiMaggio

Lance Armstrong

Michelle Kwan

Mickey Mantle

Muhammad Ali

Peyton Manning

Roberto Clemente

Sandy Koufax

Sasha Cohen

Tiger Woods

Tim Duncan

Tom Brady

Tony Dungy

Wayne Gretzky

Wilma Rudolph

Yao Ming

Sports Heroes
and *LEGENDS*™

YAOMING

by Matt Doeden

TFCB Twenty-First Century Books/Minneapolis

Twenty-First Century Books
A division of Lerner Publishing Group, Inc.
241 First Avenue North
Minneapolis, MN 55401 U.S.A.

Website address: www.lernerbooks.com

Front Cover: © Stephen Dunn/Getty Images
Back Cover: © iStockphoto.com/Bill Grove

Library of Congress Cataloging-in-Publication Data

Doeden, Matt.
    Yao Ming / by Matt Doeden.
        p. cm. — (Sports heroes and legends)
    Includes bibliographical references and index.
    ISBN 978-0-7613-4227-4 (lib. bdg. : alk. paper)
    1. Yao, Ming, 1980—Juvenile literature. 2. Basketball players—China—Biography—
Juvenile literature. 3. Basketball players—Texas—Houston—Biography—Juvenile
literature. 4. Houston Rockets (Basketball team)—Juvenile literature. I. Title.
    GV884.Y36D64 2009
    796.323092—dc22   2008051328

Manufactured in the United States of America
1 2 3 4 5 6 – JR – 14 13 12 11 10 09

Contents

Coming Up Big

Twenty-three-year-old Yao Ming still had a lot to prove when he stepped onto the court on November 17, 2002. His Houston Rockets were facing the defending champions of the National Basketball Association (NBA), the Los Angeles Lakers. The 7-foot-6 center from China had been the number one overall pick of the NBA draft just a few months earlier. Yao had dominated his competition in China, but the NBA was another story. He hadn't scored in his NBA debut and hadn't done much to excite Rockets fans in the handful of games since then. In fact, he'd scored only 30 points total in his first seven games. Some fans and reporters were starting to wonder if the Rockets had made a huge mistake.

Yao had been looking forward to playing the Lakers, mainly because he wanted to see how he matched up to the NBA's best center, Shaquille O'Neal. But Shaq was out of the

1

game with a toe injury. While this was a disappointment to Yao, Shaq's absence meant that the Lakers didn't really have anyone who could equal Yao's size and strength.

Yao started the game on the bench and watched as his teammates kept pace with the powerful Lakers. In the second quarter, Yao entered the game. Based on his play so far that season, little was expected of him. He'd looked confused and overmatched for most of his brief NBA career. But that night, it all started to come together. He got into the action right away, throwing down two strong dunks over the smaller Lakers front line. He kept pouring it on, making layups and even an acrobatic spinning reverse shot (a shot in which a player goes under the basket and scores from the opposite side of his approach).

In the fourth quarter, the Rockets trailed the Lakers by 5 points. Yao got a short rest on the bench and then checked back into the game. He quickly got into the action, scoring on a layup and then again on a hook shot.

With a minute to go, Yao had helped Houston to a 1-point lead. Houston guard Juaquin Hawkins drove the ball inside and dished off a quick pass to Yao beneath the basket. Yao caught the pass and slammed home a one-handed dunk as a Laker defender hacked him for a foul. The basket counted, and Yao got a free throw for a chance at a 3-point play. If he made the free throw, the Rockets would have a two-possession lead (meaning the Lakers couldn't tie the game with a single basket) and would be in a great position to win. Yao stepped up to the line and blocked out the screaming Lakers fans who were trying to distract him. He calmly made the free throw, and the Rockets held on for a 93–89 win. Yao had made all nine shots that he had attempted in the game and both of his free throws. With 20 points in just 23 minutes, Yao had shown the Lakers and the world that he had what it took to play in the NBA.

Shaq met Yao on the court after the game to congratulate him. "You played pretty good, Yao Ming," Shaq said.

"That's because you weren't there," Yao answered with a smile.

Yao knew that he still had plenty of work to do to establish himself as a player in the NBA. But this was a great start.

Chapter One

Big Little Yao

Yao Ming has always stood out in a crowd. Born in Shanghai, China, on September 12, 1980, he was anything but ordinary. The 23-inch, 11.2-pound baby was almost twice the size of the average Chinese newborn.

Yao's stature wasn't a total surprise, however. His mother, Fang Feng Di, towered above most men at 6 foot 3, while his father, Yao Zhi Yuan, stood 6 foot 10. Both parents were basketball players in China. Fang had been a star center on the Chinese national women's team, while Yao Zhi Yuan was a forward on Shanghai's Chinese Basketball Association (CBA) team. They were affectionately referred to as "Big Fang" and "Big Yao."

The events leading up to Yao Ming's birth are controversial. China's Communist government may have played a part in setting up the pairing between Yao's parents. Some have

4

suggested that China arranged for Yao's parents to be married in the hope that their offspring would inherit their size and athleticism, but whether that really happened is unclear. What is clear is that, decades before Yao Ming's birth, the Chinese government had taken a keen interest in the Yao family, all of whom towered over their fellow countrymen.

What's in a Name?

Written in Chinese, Yao's name is 姚 明. In Chinese, the first name (Yao) is the family name from the father's side. The second part of his name, Ming, means "light." The proper way to address Yao is by his first name alone or by his full name. Calling him just "Ming" is incorrect. When pronouncing his name, both Yao and Ming should be said with the voice inflecting upward.

Yao's parents did not wish for their son to become an athlete, however. They understood the difficulties of being an athlete in China. Chinese athletes don't earn the huge salaries awarded to professional athletes in the United States. When their playing days are over, they have to find regular jobs but usually lack the necessary skills. In many ways, former athletes were at a serious disadvantage once they stopped playing sports professionally. Yao's parents didn't want such an uncertain future for their son. Instead, they encouraged his other interests, from reading and geography to building model ships.

But for Yao, the connection to basketball was almost inevitable. By the age of four, he already stood more than 4 feet tall. By age ten, he was 5 foot 5. The government took X-rays of his hands, a technique that gives an indication of how tall a person will eventually grow. The test predicted that the boy would grow to be 7 foot 3.

In Shanghai, children were allowed to ride the bus for free, but only those under 4 foot 2. Yao shot past that mark so quickly that he says that he doesn't remember ever riding for free.

"I never felt uncomfortable with my size," Yao later wrote. "Of course, some kids made fun of me, but it didn't really bother me. Everybody has been made fun of for something."

Even with his impressive size, Yao didn't appear to be a basketball star in the making at first. He was clumsy. One basketball coach said that he'd never be a great player because his backside was too big! Yao tired quickly and moved sluggishly on the court. Even his mother doubted that her son had the makings of an athlete. "I never imagined that someone who was so stiff and ill at ease when he was little would [become a basketball star]," she later said.

When Yao was in the first grade, his class gathered for a basketball shooting contest. The teacher asked Yao to go first, knowing that his parents had both played basketball. Proudly, Yao took the ball and fired up a shot. The ball banged against the backboard and fell to the ground. He'd missed. "I was really just so embarrassed," Yao later said of his first taste of basketball.

When Yao was seven years old, he got very sick. Doctors accidentally gave him the wrong medication and he got even sicker. As a result, he permanently lost the hearing in his left ear.

Yao soon began to improve, however. At age nine, he began attending Xu Jia Hui District Youth Sports School, a specialized school that trained young athletes. His mother was hesitant to let him go, but she knew that playing basketball could help Yao get into college one day. Just as in the United States, extracurricular activities can increase a student's chances for acceptance to a university. After his embarrassing start in grade school, Yao's shooting got a lot better. He also handled the ball well, especially for someone of his size. At age thirteen, Yao was asked to try out for the Shanghai junior basketball team. (Shanghai's teams would later become known as the Sharks.) Once again, Yao's parents were reluctant to let him play. But the team's coach was a good friend, and eventually they agreed.

As a member of the junior team, Yao's life changed. Basketball became the center of his world. He and his team-mates sometimes practiced ten hours a day. And when he wasn't training for basketball, Yao briefly took up the sport of water polo.

On the court, Yao's size (he stood about 6 foot 5 by this time) made him a natural fit for the center position. But his gentle nature worked against him. He was timid and avoided the rougher play that often takes place in the painted area immediately under and in front of the basket, known as the paint. A center has to be willing to use his size and strength to overpower opposing players, but Yao wasn't yet able to do this. Because Yao was perceived as less aggressive, he spent a lot of time on the bench.

"Yao Ming was puffy," said one of his coaches. "When he first came, he was fat all over. But by practicing every day, his fat turned into muscle."

Gentle Giant

The neighborhood kids often picked on Yao. They even hit him. But Yao never fought back, despite the fact that he was bigger and stronger than any of them.

Yao's coaches and his parents worked with him. They taught him to be tougher and to use his strength to his advantage. Before long, Yao was starting—and starring—for the team. As his skills began to catch up with his size, he began to get attention from NBA teams. At age sixteen, 7-foot-2 Yao went to a Nike basketball camp held in Paris, France. It was his first trip outside China. There he got a taste of what Western-style basketball was like. It was clear that being a star in China didn't mean that he could keep up with the best international players in his age group. Yao still had a long way to go.

Later that year, Yao broke his foot. He was jumping to collect a rebound and landed awkwardly on another player's foot. The play marked the end of his junior career. When the foot was healed, he was promoted to the Sharks' senior team.

In 1997, seventeen-year-old Yao entered his rookie season with the Sharks' senior team. He and his teammates competed in China's eighth National Games, a gathering of top teams that took place before the beginning of the regular CBA season. In one of the first games, the Sharks hosted the mighty Bayi Rockets, who had long dominated the CBA. One of the opposing players was Wang Zhizhi, a young player considered by many to be the best in China. Wang was three years older than Yao, who had been compared to the older boy ever since he'd started playing. Yao came off the bench in the game and blocked one of Wang's shots almost right away, to the delight of the crowd. Then he blocked another one. Wang and the Rockets won the game, but Yao had proven that he had what it took to play with China's best.

Playing wasn't easy for Yao early on, however. In one game, he played 40 minutes and scored 19 points before coming off the floor, breathing heavily and announcing that he couldn't play anymore.

"In those days, [Yao] had the height and agility, but he was too frail and didn't have enough ball skills," said his coach, Lu Zhiqiang. "He was only able to stand beneath the basket and defend."

He went on to average 10 points and 8.3 rebounds during the CBA's regular season, while the Sharks finished fifth out of twelve teams.

In the summer of 1998, Yao and his friend and teammate Liu Wei traveled to the United States for the first time to attend a basketball camp called High Five America. There, Yao got a taste of American culture and learned more about playing a rougher, tougher, Western style of basketball. His coach told him to dunk the ball every chance he got. If Yao got the ball down low (meaning his teammates gave him good passes near the basket) and didn't dunk it, the coach made the team run laps. That focus on aggressive play was just one example of how basketball in China was different from the game played in the United States. Yao learned to be aggressive with the ball at all times. Those who saw him play were stunned, and by the end of the camp he was ranked second among the forty centers in attendance.

EATING ON A BUDGET

Yao brought only $200 with him on his first trip to the United States in the summer of 1998. He had to live on that amount for two months. So he ate 99-cent fast-food cheeseburgers and filled up on complimentary breakfasts offered by the team's hotels.

Reporter Robin Miller saw Yao play and was impressed. "His name is Yao Ming, and on the basketball court he is the eighth wonder of the world," Miller wrote. "He's 7 feet, 5 inches tall, weighs 252 pounds, has an arm span of 9 feet 3 inches, and can make 15-foot jump shots with agility.... Compared with these other young basketball players he stands out like a crane among chickens."

"That summer, I began to think maybe I really could play in the NBA," Yao later said.

Yao tried out for the Chinese junior national team that was headed to the 1998 Asian Games but was cut from the roster. This was a bitter disappointment for him since he badly wanted to represent his country.

"At that time, his spirit hit rock bottom," said Yao's teammate Liu Wei.

Yao's disappointment wouldn't last long, however. His game was about to take a giant step forward.

Chapter Two

China's Star Center

Yao truly began to come into his own in his second full season with the Sharks' senior squad. He missed ten games early in the season with another broken foot. Without him, the Sharks struggled badly. But when Yao returned to the team's lineup on February 3, 1999, he made an immediate impact, scoring 17 points and leading Shanghai to an overtime victory over Beijing.

Yao went on to average 20.9 points in the final twelve games of the season. The Sharks' 12–10 record was good enough to earn them a playoff spot, but they lost to Guangdong in the playoff series. Yao was so disappointed after one tough loss to Guangdong that he was in tears. All the news wasn't bad, however. Yao was named the CBA's most improved player for his efforts even though he'd missed almost half the season.

A few months later, Yao was asked to join the national team to participate in the Asian Men's Basketball Championship, to be held in Japan. The tournament was important for China. They had to win it to qualify for a spot in the 2000 Olympic Games in Sydney, Australia.

The Chinese team was heavily favored in the tournament. Their front line, with Wang and Mengke Bateer as forwards and Yao at center, was an impressive unit. Experts predicted that China would blow out an overmatched Malaysian team in the tournament's first game. But the small, quick Malaysian team gave China a lot of trouble. Yao and his teammates managed a 54–41 win, which was far closer than anyone had expected. They'd have to play a lot better if they wanted to win the tournament and secure a place in the Olympics. Yao and his teammates came back strong, dominating Syria 112–61 and Kuwait 91–54. In that game, Yao scored 20 points and connected on all nine of his shots from the field (non–free throws). In the championship game, China defeated Korea to claim the title. Yao would be headed to the Olympics in 2000!

But first, Yao and the Sharks had to focus on the CBA season. Yao's skills continued to evolve. In a game late in 1999, he racked up five fouls in the first half. One more foul would put him out of the game. But Yao played most of the second half without committing another foul, and the Sharks won 88–81.

Despite that win, the team was struggling to live up to expectations. "We were playing very sloppily and . . . our minds weren't focused enough," Yao later said.

The Sharks turned their season around in the second half and made the playoffs. But once again, few expected them to compete for the title. Yao averaged 21.2 points per game during the regular season, which was impressive, but the Sharks were still not on a par with the CBA's top teams. The Sharks heated things up in the playoffs, however, and defeated Beijing and Guangdong, earning them a trip to the championship series. There, they'd face Wang and the Bayi Rockets, who had dominated the Sharks over the years. The championship would be a best-of-five series, meaning the first team to get three wins would earn the title.

The opening game was a back-and-forth struggle. The Sharks were ahead after the first quarter, but an injury to guard Liu Wei slowed them down. Bayi surged to a 15-point halftime lead and then held on for an easy 116–94 win. Yao scored 21 points and had 17 rebounds, but it wasn't nearly enough.

Early in the second game, things seemed even worse. The Sharks fell behind 20–4 and seemed unable to compete with the powerful Rockets. But at that point, Yao and his teammates caught fire. They stormed back and took a 55–54 lead at halftime. The teams stayed close throughout the third quarter. But by the fourth quarter, Yao had played every minute of the game and was exhausted. The Sharks had spent all of their energy in the furious comeback, and Bayi took control late in the game for the win. In the final game, the Rockets finished off the Sharks and won another championship.

"We have won second place in the league championship, which we have long craved," Yao said after the final loss. "But this is not the final goal of the team. We will continue to exert ourselves to win the overall championship [soon]."

Yao didn't have to wait for the 2000–2001 season to find the spotlight again, however. In September 2000, he traveled to Sydney, Australia, with his teammates to participate in the Olympic Games. Experts weren't sure what to expect out of the Chinese team and their "Moving Great Wall" of Yao, Wang, and Bateer. Could they compete with teams that played fast-paced, aggressive, Western-style basketball? They certainly had the size along the front line, but would their guards be able to match up?

The Chinese philosophy was that practice—and lots of it—was the key to success. But they may have overdone it before the Olympics, playing game after game while other teams rested. As a result, the Chinese team looked tired right from the start. To make matters worse, their first opponent was the United States and its Dream Team of NBA stars. The U.S. team's starting lineup of Jason Kidd, Gary Payton, Vince Carter,

Kevin Garnett, and Alonzo Mourning was intimidating for any team and was heavily favored to win the gold medal.

At least publicly, the U.S. team didn't seem too worried about China's team. Before the game, the U.S. players were putting on a high-flying show for the spectators rather than going through the usual warm-ups.

But once the game started, the Chinese team was all business, building a surprising 13–7 lead in the early minutes. The U.S. team seemed determined to score in the paint but was surprised by Yao's solid defense. In one sequence, Yao blocked a Garnett shot and then blocked Carter on the next possession. The arena erupted in support for Yao and the underdog Chinese team. Could China possibly be good enough to compete with, or even beat, the powerful Americans?

The U.S. team kept pounding the ball inside in an effort to draw fouls on the Chinese big men. The tactic worked. Wang quickly picked up four fouls and had to go to the bench to avoid fouling out. With Wang out, the U.S. defense could focus on Yao, denying him the ball down low. They also got him in foul trouble, and he fouled out early in the second half. With Yao out of the game, China's hopes disappeared and the American team rolled to an easy 112–79 victory.

"[The Chinese team was] fearless, not afraid of anybody," Carter said after the game. "They were really into it, and this is the kind of opponent I like to compete with, because it makes the game more fun."

The Chinese team didn't play much better after that. The players looked tired and sluggish as they finished with a 2–4 record and missed the medal round of play. This poor finish was bitterly disappointing for a team that had hoped to compete for a medal. But Yao had played well, his confidence soared, and talk of his eventual move to the NBA increased.

The U.S. Dream Team went on to win Olympic gold in Sydney, defeating France 85–75 in the gold-medal game.

Yao's confidence continued to grow during the 2000–2001 CBA season. At one point, the Sharks won eleven straight games. Yao was dominant, averaging 27.1 points and 19.4 rebounds and winning the league's Most Valuable Player (MVP) award. The Sharks easily made the playoffs and advanced to the championship series. Their opponent was a familiar foe, the Bayi Rockets.

The best-of-five series opened on March 11, 2001, in Shanghai. For a change, Shanghai was favored to beat a Bayi team that some considered past its prime. But Bayi wasn't ready to give up and opened an early 20–10 lead. The Sharks focused on defense and quickly closed the gap to 4 points at halftime. In the second half, Yao kept attacking the basket. His aggressive play forced Wang into committing fouls, and the Bayi star soon had to go to the bench with foul trouble. With Wang on the bench, the Sharks took control and earned a close victory.

The Rockets came back to win the second game of the series, largely because Yao spent all of the second half in foul trouble, so he couldn't play aggressive defense against Wang. In the third game, Yao took the court sporting a bandage above one of his eyes to cover a cut suffered in the previous day's practice. The scrape didn't slow him down, however. He played tenacious defense under the basket, blocking shots and forcing turnovers. The Rockets responded by switching to an outside game, trying to prevent Yao from making a strong impact. The strategy worked, and the Rockets took a 2-point lead into the fourth quarter. The Sharks looked frustrated on the court, and Bayi took advantage with a 131–122 victory and a 2–1 lead in the series.

The Sharks were in trouble. They needed to win Game 4 to force a winner-take-all Game 5. But it wasn't to be. The Rockets used a brilliant outside shooting performance to build a big second-half lead; the Sharks just couldn't keep up. With the 128–118 victory, Bayi had yet another title. Once again, the Sharks had managed just second place.

❝I really didn't expect Yao Ming to have improved so much this year. Now all the Shanghai team needs is Yao Ming on the inside, and because of [his] superiority under the basket, the other players can go out to guard . . . the perimeter. Offensively, Yao Ming takes up a lot of our defensive strength . . . which puts a lot of pressure on our outside [defense].**❞**

—BAYI GUARD LI NAN DURING THE 2001
SHARKS-ROCKETS PLAYOFF SERIES

The 2001–2002 season would be Yao's last with the Sharks and the CBA. Already, the wheels were in motion to bring him to the United States and the NBA. This would be his last chance to lead Shanghai to a CBA title, and he wasn't about to let the opportunity slip away. Yao dominated the league like no player had ever done before, averaging 32.4 points and 19.0 rebounds per game during the regular season. The Sharks were often ahead by so much that Yao spent most of the second half on the bench resting. The team cruised to the top regular-season record and then to the championship series. To the surprise of no one, they would face Bayi for the third straight time. Could Shanghai finally knock out the defending champs?

Wang had moved on to the NBA, so the Sharks were heavily favored. The Rockets had a good outside game but no one who could challenge Yao's size and strength under the basket. In spite of that, Bayi surged to a big lead of 19 points in the first game.

WANG PAVES THE WAY

In 1999, the Dallas Mavericks took Wang Zhizhi in the second round of the NBA draft with the 36th pick overall. In 2001, Wang finally joined the team for five games. He returned in 2001–2002, when he played in 55 games and averaged 5.6 points per game. Wang bounced around the league for several more years but never made a real impact.

Yao and the Sharks came back and tied the game 85–85 late in the third quarter. From there, the game was a thrilling back-and-forth affair. The teams traded basket after basket. With less than a minute to play in the fourth quarter, the Rockets led by 2 points. Yao got the ball down low and went up for a shot.

His defender hacked at him as he made the shot, giving him a free throw and a chance for a 3-point play. To the delight of the Shanghai fans, he knocked down the free throw to give the Sharks a 125–124 lead. But the Rockets weren't done. Guard Li Nan hit a big three-pointer, then the Sharks turned the ball over, and, just like that, the game was over. Once again, the Rockets had come out on top, 127–125. Amazingly, Yao had made 21 of 21 shots in the game for a career-high 49 points. But in the end, his strong play hadn't been enough.

The Sharks won Game 2 by a score of 124–92, led by Yao's 26 points and 23 rebounds. After the game, in a TV interview, Yao said, "The Bayi Rockets are old. They can't play with us."

The boast was unusual. Yao and most Chinese players rarely say such things about their opponents. In fact, it's customary for players and coaches to say that the other team is better and should win the game. But Yao wanted to give his teammates confidence. The tactic worked. The Sharks won again in Game 3, 129–122 (Yao scored 46 points), which meant that they were just one win away from claiming their first CBA title. But the final two games of the series would be played in Bayi's home arena, where they'd won an amazing sixty-six straight games. To win the title, the Sharks would have to end that streak.

Game 4 was held on April 19. It was another tight contest, with the teams trading the lead back and forth late into the fourth quarter. With just 32 seconds left, the game was tied 119–119. Yao took a pass and muscled his way inside, making a shot to give the Sharks the lead. Then Bayi's Liu Yudong launched a three-pointer that swooshed through the net. The Rockets were ahead 122–121, just 7.6 seconds remained on the clock, and the Bayi fans were ready to celebrate a big win.

The Sharks got the ball to Yao, but his shot rimmed out. A follow-up shot also missed. But with just one second to go, an American player for the Sharks named Steve Hart rose up and put the ball through the basket. The final buzzer sounded as Yao and his teammates celebrated the thrilling 123–122 victory. They were the CBA champions!

After the title, Yao apologized for his earlier remarks about Bayi. "The Bayi Rockets are not really too old," he said. "They taught [us] a lot. I'm sorry I said that. I just wanted our players to believe we could beat them."

The win was a memorable finish to the season. It would also be Yao's last game as a member of the Shanghai Sharks. A new challenge awaited him in the United States.

Chapter | Three

The Road to the NBA

In April 2002, Yao's dreams were coming true. He had finally achieved his goal of leading the Sharks to the CBA championship. And that same month, Yao got permission from the Chinese government to follow Wang to the NBA. After years of fans and the media talking about Yao playing in the United States, the move was finally about to happen. Yao was going to be just the second Chinese player in NBA history.

There wasn't much time for Yao to rest. The NBA draft was coming up, and teams wanted to see Yao work out. Less than two weeks after winning the CBA title, Yao flew to Chicago, Illinois, to show his stuff. Because he was largely an unknown entering the draft, there was plenty of speculation on when he would be selected and by whom. Wang had struggled in the NBA, which led some to believe that Yao might have trouble too. On the other hand, Yao was 7 foot 6 and strong, and had good basketball skills—an extremely rare combination.

In his first workout, at a small, private session for the teams that had shown the strongest interest in him, Yao showed off his shooting skills. He was on fire, hitting 80 percent of his shots and knocking down all of the mid-range jumpers he attempted. Mid-range jump shots are taken from about 15 feet away and are typically outside the comfortable range of many NBA centers. The NBA scouts in attendance were impressed.

In his next workout, Yao performed before dozens of scouts and journalists as well as thousands of fans who were eager to see what the big Chinese man could do. Yao later admitted that he'd been tired during the workout and hadn't done his best, but he'd shown enough to impress everyone watching.

"There wasn't any one thing he did that made you go 'Wow,'" said former NBA coach P. J. Carlesimo. "It was just the sum total [of his skills]. He could put the ball on the floor, run, shoot, pass, and, oh yeah, he's 7 foot 6 and 300 pounds. . . . If you watched for ten minutes, you knew he was going to be a force in the NBA."

That spring, the NBA held its annual lottery to determine the draft order. The NBA uses a system in which all the non-playoff teams from the previous season take part in a random draw of marked Ping-Pong balls for the top picks. The team with the worst record has the most Ping-Pong balls, the second-worst team has the second-most Ping-Pong balls, and so on. The team whose ball is picked first gets the top overall pick. The Houston Rockets, whose 28–54 record had been the league's fifth worst during the 2001–2002 season, won the lottery, which gave them the first overall pick in the draft. The Chicago Bulls, who had long shown an interest in Yao, drew the second pick.

In the spring of 2002, Yao started dating Ye Li, a player on China's women's national team. The couple spent as much time together as they could.

The Rockets were very interested in Yao. But Houston officials also knew that drafting Yao would come with complications. They still had to get the Sharks' formal approval for Yao to leave. That had seemed all but assured, but Wang Zhizhi, who had just finished his rookie season with the Dallas Mavericks, had said that he didn't want to return to China to play with the national team despite an earlier agreement to do so. Wang's decision worried the Chinese since they wondered whether Yao would make the same choice. There were also rumors that Yao wanted to play for the Chicago Bulls, not for the Rockets. Yao said that the rumors were untrue. A third concern was Yao's health. X-rays of his feet showed damage from the breaks he'd suffered during his CBA career.

Erik Zhang, a friend of one of Yao's cousins living in the United States, helped Yao deal with the complicated situation. Zhang talked to the Rockets on Yao's behalf and later worked on contract negotiations. He, along with several others, including Yao's formal agent, John Huizinga, constituted Team Yao.

Eventually, all of the roadblocks were removed. The Sharks and the Chinese government gave Yao and the Rockets their blessing. The Rockets agreed that Yao could play for the Chinese national team during important international events, such as the Olympics. Yao also agreed to send a percentage of his salary back to China.

Yao went to Houston for a private workout and got a chance to know head coach Rudy Tomjanovich. Finally, on June 26, the NBA draft arrived. To the surprise of no one, the Rockets formally selected Yao with the first overall pick. Yao watched the draft from China, where he was training with the national team. Wearing a Rockets hat, he celebrated with his parents and then did a TV interview for the TNT network, which broadcasted the draft.

"There will be many challenges in the NBA, and many difficulties," said the number one pick. "I think the most important thing is . . . to go there and learn, so that our country's level in basketball can be raised even further."

Yao spoke in Chinese, with a translator, for many of his post-draft interviews. But he also showed that he could speak some English. A Houston reporter asked him to say hello to the Rockets fans in English. Yao didn't miss a beat, answering in English, "I am very happy to join the Houston Rockets. Hi! Houston, I'm coming."

The contract negotiations began almost right away. The Rockets had to deal with both Yao and the Sharks, which still held his rights in China. The Rockets agreed to give the Sharks ten major gifts, including cash, help in finding new foreign players, and help in training their current players and coaching staff. The Rockets and Team Yao also had to agree on a contract for Yao himself. Eventually, Yao signed a four-year deal worth $18 million.

But before he could start his NBA career, Yao had to play with the Chinese team in the World Championships. Before the tournament, which was held in Indianapolis, Indiana, the Chinese team played an exhibition game against Canada. Many NBA fans had seen Yao play in the 2000 Olympics, so they knew who he was. The Chinese team struggled, but Yao gave the crowd what they'd come to see. He got the ball down low, under the basket. Canada's center, Richard Anderson, leaned on Yao, playing tough defense. But Yao quickly faked going one way, then spun the other way. He jumped up to take the shot. Anderson raked his hands across Yao's arms, but Yao was too strong. He slammed the ball through the hoop as the referee called a foul on Anderson. Yao took the free throw to complete an impressive 3-point play.

Unfortunately, Yao's good play wasn't enough. The Chinese guards couldn't keep up with the quick, talented Canadians, led by NBA star Steve Nash. Canada cruised to an easy 94–66 victory.

During the World Championships in 2002, *Sports Illustrated* magazine featured Yao on the cover with the headline "The Next Big Thing."

The World Championships were more of the same. The Chinese team struggled, while Yao excelled. He averaged 21 points and was named to the all-tournament team. At the Asian Games, the heavily favored Chinese team advanced to the finals and appeared to be on its way to its fifth-straight gold medal. China led South Korea by 7 points with a minute to go in the title game. But then everything fell apart. South Korea put together a shocking comeback to win 102–100, despite Yao's 23 points and 22 rebounds.

Yao was disappointed, but the NBA season was approaching. On October 19, Yao left China for the United States. He was ready to join his new team.

THINKING GLOBALLY

A reporter at the World Championships asked Yao how he hoped to be remembered when his pro career was done. He replied, "I don't know exactly which words to use to accurately express it, but I hope that through me [people] will have a greater interest in basketball, that they will know that this is a great sport worthy of involvement. This is what I would like people to remember and understand through me."

Chapter Four

NBA Rookie

Yao joined the Rockets with the NBA season only ten days away. The other players had been together in training camp for weeks. The Asian Games and contract difficulties had kept Yao away, which meant that he had to hit the ground running. He had to learn the team's plays and how to work with his teammates while adapting to life in the United States. The changes and pressures were a lot for the twenty-three-year-old to take in.

Yao's teammates embraced him. Houston's star guard Steve Francis was among the first to befriend the rookie center. "I could tell [Yao] was scared in that first practice," Francis said. "He didn't want all those cameras looking at him. He didn't know how to come talk to the guys. . . . He was just trying to ease in, but you could tell he didn't feel comfortable."

So Francis made sure that Yao was involved with the other players during practice. After the team was done, Francis took

Yao out to a local golf course for a lunch and golf event with Houston season-ticket holders. Yao and Francis got along well, which was a big relief. Francis was the leader of the team, so if Yao could get along with Francis, he should be okay with the rest of the team.

Basketball was just one challenge that Yao faced in a new country. Even with translator Colin Pine at his side, communication was a constant struggle. Yao also learned how to drive and how to deal with the aggressive American media. His dealings with the media have, at times, been humorous. Once when asked what the easiest part about living in the United States was, Yao answered simply, "Sleeping."

Yao's teammates always tried to make him feel at home. In January 2003, they held a Chinese New Year party for him, with lots of Chinese decorations and Chinese music. They even mimicked a Chinese tradition by giving Yao red envelopes with small amounts of cash inside.

Yao's first preseason game was on October 23 against the San Antonio Spurs and David Robinson and Tim Duncan, who were known as the Twin Towers. Yao played some good defense but also got himself into foul trouble almost right away. He scored 6 points in the 80–79 loss.

❝[Yao] is the biggest individual sports story in the world. There are 2 billion Asian people, and everybody's watching it. . . . In two years, he'll be bigger than Michael [Jordan] ever was, and bigger than Tiger [Woods]. I think he's going to be the number one icon in the world.❞
—HOUSTON ROCKETS OWNER LESLIE ALEXANDER JUST BEFORE THE 2002–2003 NBA SEASON

The real test came a week later. The Rockets opened their regular season against the Indiana Pacers in Indianapolis on October 30. Even though the game was between two teams not expected to contend for a title, there was nationwide, even worldwide, interest in the game. Everyone wanted to see how the big Chinese player would fare against NBA competition.

Yao spent the entire first quarter on the bench. Finally, in the second quarter, he got his chance. The Pacers quickly passed the ball down low, probably to test Yao. Yao committed a foul, which was not how he'd hoped to start out, and his play didn't get any better. Yao looked sluggish and lost during his eleven minutes of play. He missed the only shot he took and finished the game scoreless. The Rockets lost 91–82.

Things didn't get much better in the next few games. In the second game, against the Denver Nuggets, Yao managed to get his first NBA points. He took the ball and did a spin move to the baseline, fooling his defender and giving Yao an easy layup. They were his only points of the night, though the Rockets did win the game. Point totals of 8 and 0 in his next two games did little to increase his confidence.

In Yao's sixth NBA game, against the Portland Trailblazers, he got a chance to play against one of his heroes, center Arvydas Sabonis. Yao had admired Sabonis for years and even used Sabonis as one of his screen names when he played computer games online.

By this time, many fans and reporters had started to wonder whether Yao really belonged in the NBA. Former NBA star Charles Barkley, who worked for the TNT television network, predicted that Yao wouldn't score as many as 19 points in a game all season. Others said that the Rockets had made a big mistake and had wasted the top pick in the draft. Yao was compared to other big draft busts, including the 1993 second-overall pick, Shawn Bradley, a big man who never made much impact in the league.

Yao answered his critics with a 20-point performance against the Lakers in his eighth game of the season, making all nine shots he took from the field and going 2–2 from the free-throw line. Two games later, he did even better against the undefeated Dallas Mavericks. The Mavericks were one of the few teams in the league who had a center who could match Yao's height. Shawn Bradley wasn't known as an offensive star, but his defense had always been solid. Yao was almost unstoppable, especially early on. He scored 21 points in the first half alone and netted 30 for the game on 10-of-12 shooting. He also dominated the boards, collecting 16 rebounds. He even added 2 blocked shots for good measure. Unfortunately, Yao's stellar performance wasn't enough since the rest of the team fell flat. Dallas won the game 108–90.

"I definitely had more confidence tonight," Yao said. "From a technical standpoint, I felt very good. I played a lot of minutes today. Of course, I want to play more. But I have to build up my endurance."

It was an up-and-down season, both for Yao and the Rockets. Yao followed up his 30-point performance with 18 against Michael Jordan and the Washington Wizards but then managed just 4 points against Wang Zhizhi and the Los Angeles Clippers. He was showing flashes of brilliance. During an eight-game stretch in December, he averaged 19.5 points and 14.3 rebounds, including 27 and 18 against San Antonio and their Twin Towers. While these were All-Star-caliber numbers, he still came across at times like a rookie player who was uncertain of himself on the court. In January, Yao scored fewer than 11 points in all but 1 of 11 games.

One of those games was against the Lakers—this time with a healthy Shaq. The game got a lot of media coverage because leading up to it, Shaq had made a joke about Yao by speaking in a fake Chinese accent. Shaq's words angered many people, despite the fact that Yao accepted it as just a joke. Yao scored just 10 points in the game, but he also blocked 6 shots. He made a big impression in the opening minutes, blocking one of Shaq's shots and going down the court to throw down a dunk of his own. Once again, the Rockets managed to defeat the defending champs, 108–104.

One of Yao's more memorable moments of the season occurred in a game against the Atlanta Hawks on January 10. Atlanta center Theo Ratliff had been playing tough defense. He was frustrating Yao, who missed his first seven shots. Finally, in the third quarter, Yao got the ball deep and took out his frustration with a rim-rattling, two-handed dunk on Ratliff. Yao let it all out with a celebratory shout, and the referee quickly blew the whistle for a technical foul. Yao's teammates hooted and hollered from the bench. It was exactly the kind of emotion they wanted to see from the normally reserved rookie.

"I learned something from that game and that technical," Yao later wrote in his autobiography, *Yao: A Life in Two Worlds.* "You have to be tough when the playing is tough. If the other team plays hard, you can play harder."

On March 21, 2003, against the Golden State Warriors, Yao made the first and only 3-point shot of his career (through the 2007–2008 season).

NBA fans were taking notice of Yao's unique talents and voted him as the starting center for the Western Conference in the All-Star game in a narrow victory over Shaq. The game was held in Atlanta, and all eyes were on Yao. He didn't disappoint. Early in the game, he took a pass from Francis and threw down an alley-oop dunk, igniting the crowd. The Western Conference won 155–145 in double overtime, but Yao hadn't played a lot in the game. Shaq and Duncan logged most of the minutes at center. But being voted as a starter was an indication of just how popular Yao was. Even as a rookie, Yao was a player who people wanted to see.

Yao's likable personality and worldwide recognition made him an instant hit with advertisers. He starred in several television commercials during his first seasons in the NBA, including a spot for Apple computers costarring with 2-foot-8 actor Verne Troyer.

The NBA's Western Conference was by far stronger than its Eastern Conference. The Rockets did all they could to stay in the playoff race, but teams such as the Lakers, Spurs, Mavericks, Minnesota Timberwolves, and Sacramento Kings dominated. This left a bunch of teams fighting for the remaining three play-off spots. The Rockets' record was split at 30 wins, 30 losses in early March. The team needed to push to secure a playoff berth. Teams had really started to focus on defending Yao, making it more and more difficult for him to make shots. The Rockets also had to cope with some bad news. Coach Tomjanovich had been diagnosed with cancer and had to spend time away from the team. In the end, all of this and the team's inexperience proved to be too much to overcome. The Rockets finished the season at 42–40. Thy had a winning record but didn't earn a playoff spot.

The emergence of Yao, along with the stellar play of Francis, gave Rockets fans plenty of hope for the future, however. After the season, Amare Stoudemire, the Phoenix Suns forward, narrowly beat out Yao for the NBA's Rookie of the Year award. Yao had averaged 13.5 points and 8.2 rebounds in the season, but exhaustion had taken its toll on him. After all, counting the previous CBA season and all the games with the Chinese national team, he'd been playing almost nonstop for a year and a half. He probably could have used a summer off to rest his body. But with his commitment to the Chinese national team, that wasn't to be. Yao had more basketball to play.

Chapter Five

Wall-to-Wall Basketball

Yao was eager to return to China. The nation was suffering from an outbreak of a disease called severe acute respiratory syndrome, or SARS. Yao did all he could to help SARS victims. He used his celebrity to raise money through a telethon. His teammate Steve Francis, along with other NBA players, including Jordan and Shaq, took part by appearing in a video for the telethon.

Many NBA players use the off-season to relax and get away from basketball for a month or two. That wasn't an option for Yao. He'd made commitments to the Chinese national team, and he intended to fulfill them. The team started the summer by playing exhibition games to prepare for the 2003 Asian Championship games. Yao's experience in the NBA paid off for the whole team. He'd discovered new ways of looking at the game and new ways of practicing. He brought them back to the team, hoping to help Chinese basketball get one step closer to the level played in the West. At one point, Yao and his teammates played (and won) nine games in two weeks—hardly a rest after a long NBA season! The Chinese fans often mobbed Yao. Everyone wanted to meet him or get an autograph.

As expected, Yao and the Chinese team won the Asian Championships (defeating South Korea) and qualified for the 2004 Olympics. Yao was named MVP of the tournament. He was thrilled to have helped China qualify for the Olympics, but he was exhausted. His doctors diagnosed him with high blood pressure. He should have rested during the off-season, but his obligations made it impossible. So he took a stand. He told the Chinese that he would happily play in tournaments, but he wouldn't play more than three warm-up games before a tournament.

"I always thought I could play in the NBA until age thirty-five," he said. "But if I continue like this, every day of the NBA season, followed by Chinese training and all of the off-the-court social activities, I won't have time to rest at all. Maybe I will have to retire at age thirty."

When Yao returned to the United States and the Rockets in October, he had a new head coach, Jeff Van Gundy. Tomjanovich had retired because of his health problems. With a year of experience under his belt and the emergence of teammates Francis and Cuttino Mobley, the Rockets were one of the league's up-and-coming teams. In the previous season, little had been expected of them, but in 2003–2004, fans hoped to see the team compete in the powerful Western Conference.

The Rockets started the season with a bang, winning the opening game over the Nuggets 102–85. They stayed hot early on, winning five of their first six games. Yao played well, but not spectacularly, at the start of the season. Then, in late January, he really stepped up his game. He scored 29 points against the New York Knicks on January 21 and followed that up with 37 points against the Orlando Magic two games later.

NBA fans noticed some big changes in Yao. He had been lifting weights, which was something Chinese basketball players rarely did. He was stronger than ever and was learning to use his newfound power down low to score baskets and pull down tough rebounds.

"Now I know you can't always go around [a defender]," Yao explained. "Sometimes—maybe most times—you have to go through the other player."

During the 2003–2004 season, Yao got a new set of wheels. He treated himself to a BMW 745i custom made to fit his huge frame.

Yao's best game of the season came on February 22 against the Hawks. Atlanta wasn't one of the NBA's best teams, but they played Houston tough that night. The Rockets needed a big game out of their star center, and Yao gave them exactly that.

The game was hard and bruising. The Hawks tried to focus on stopping Yao, using a zone defense designed to force play to the outside (and away from Yao). In addition, Atlanta used two big men, Joel Przybilla and Zeljko Rebraca, to punish Yao down low in hopes of wearing him down.

"They were using a lot of strategy against me that I didn't really like," Yao said. "They were doing a lot of hitting. I didn't like the way they were playing me."

With about 20 seconds to play in the game, the Rockets led 92–91. Yao took a pass down low and dropped it in for a layup. The Houston fans cheered, but the game wasn't over yet. Atlanta's Chris Crawford came right back to hit a three-pointer that sent the game into overtime. Atlanta almost won it in the first overtime, but Francis hit a shot with two seconds to play to tie it once again. In the second overtime, the Rockets were in trouble, this time down by 3 points in the final seconds. But Houston guard Jim Jackson knocked down a 3-pointer with 5 seconds to go. The game was headed to triple overtime!

That was when Yao took over. Both Przybilla and Rebraca had fouled out of the game, so he could dominate the paint. Yao scored the Rockets' first 6 points of the period, then knocked down a big jump shot near the end to tie the game. Mobley made two free throws with 8 seconds left to give Houston the lead, and this time it was for good. Yao and his teammates had just won the longest NBA game played in three years. Yao had scored a career-high 41 points in the game. He'd also collected 16 rebounds and 7 assists.

"I was very tired," he said of the marathon game. "I was tired to the point I felt numb. But I just had to keep going."

In 2004, Yao was voted the starting center of the Western Conference All-Stars for the second straight season. He scored 16 points in the West's 136–132 win.

The playoff push was on. A five-game winning streak in early March pushed Houston's record to 39–26. They cooled off down the stretch, coasting to a final mark of 45–37, but that was good enough to earn the number-seven seed (ranking) in the Western Conference. Yao was about to get his first taste of NBA playoff action, and he'd be playing against a familiar foe—the Los Angeles Lakers.

The Lakers were starting four players who were almost certain to be future Hall of Famers: Shaq, guards Kobe Bryant and Gary Payton, and forward Karl Malone. They had the second-best record in the Western Conference and were a team loaded with talent and playoff experience. So when the best-of-seven series opened in Los Angeles on April 17, many experts expected a blowout. But Yao and the Rockets had other ideas.

Francis led the Houston offense while Yao anchored the defense, more than holding his own against Shaq. After trailing by 6 points at halftime, the Rockets used their smothering defense to hold Los Angeles to just 9 third-quarter points, taking a 2-point lead. In the end, however, the Lakers had just enough to pull it out. Trailing by a point with 17 seconds left, Shaq grabbed a rebound. Yao went up to stop Shaq, but he had no chance. Shaq slammed the ball home to give Los Angeles the lead, and Yao fouled out of the game in the process. The 72–71 loss was bitterly disappointing for the Rockets. Yao scored just 10 points, hitting just 4 of 11 field goals, in his NBA playoff debut.

Los Angeles followed up the win with a convincing 98–84 victory in Game 2. Yao played better offensively, scoring 21 points, but his play wasn't enough. The series moved to Houston for the next three games, and Rockets fans were eager to see their team get into the win column. The Rockets didn't let their fans down.

Francis and Yao led the team to a 13-point halftime lead in Game 3 and never looked back. Yao scored 18 points on 9 of 13 shooting and added 10 rebounds in a 102–91 Rockets victory.

The win gave the team a chance to even the series at two games apiece two nights later. Things didn't look good after three quarters, however, with the Lakers leading 69–59. That was when the Rocket offense came alive, and its defense began to shut down the Lakers. The team fought back to tie the game 81–81 and force overtime. Yao gave the Rockets an early overtime lead when he knocked down a 20-foot jump shot. By the middle of the 5-minute overtime, the Rockets held an 87–83 lead. But Malone drew Yao's sixth foul with a minute and a half to play, and the Lakers dominated from that point forward, winning 92–88.

Yao published his autobiography, *Yao: A Life in Two Worlds*, in 2004 with the help of sports reporter Ric Bucher. At the end of the book, he added a long list of his dreams for the future. They included to live in Hawaii someday, to go bungee jumping, to help China improve the way it selects its young athletes, to carry the Chinese flag at the Olympic opening ceremonies, and to win an NBA championship.

Down 3–1 in the series, the Rockets' chances looked dim. Houston would have to win three in a row, and two of those wins would have to come in Los Angeles. At first in Game 5, they looked up to the challenge, taking a 1-point lead into half-time. But the Lakers outscored them 25–9 in a disastrous third quarter that ended the series and Houston's season.

"We were originally floating and we slowly started sinking," Yao said through his interpreter of the third-quarter collapse. It summed up the night well.

Yao had had a very good second season. His averages of 17.5 points and 9 rebounds per game were steps in the right direction, and he'd been a big part of getting Houston back to the playoffs. The summer of 2004 brought change to the team, as well as another chance for Yao to play in the Summer Olympics.

Chapter Six

On the World Stage

The Rockets weren't content to stand pat with the team they had. When star guard Tracy McGrady of the Orlando Magic demanded a trade, Houston worked hard to make a deal. Other teams, including the Phoenix Suns and Indiana Pacers, were also trying to trade for McGrady. But the star guard pushed for a Houston trade, mainly because he wanted to team up with Yao. Meanwhile, the Rockets hoped that the two-time NBA scoring champion could help push the team into the elite of the Western Conference.

In late June 2004, the trade was finalized. But in any sport, a team has to give up something to get something back. And to get McGrady, the Rockets had to give up Steve Francis, Cuttino Mobley, and Kelvin Cato. Yao lost some close friends on the team, but he gained an exciting, dynamic new team-mate in McGrady.

McGrady compared himself and Yao to the combination of Kobe Bryant and Shaq. "Seeing Kobe and how much freedom he has because of Shaq, that's really what I need to win a championship," he said. "[The Rockets] have a great coach in Jeff Van Gundy and they are going to do the things there to put the right pieces around me and Yao so we can win a championship."

Yao probably should have had a rest before gearing up to play alongside McGrady. But there simply wasn't time. He was getting ready to lead China's national team to the 2004 Olympics in Athens, Greece. For years, Yao had dreamed about carrying China's flag at the opening ceremonies of the Olympics. In Athens, his dream came true. Yao proudly led China's delegation of 407 athletes into Olympic Stadium.

❝Yao . . . represents a good image of Chinese athletes. He is a man of integrity and has a good sense of humor. He is the perfect one to be the flag-bearer.**❞**
— XIAO TIAN, SECRETARY GENERAL OF THE 2004 CHINESE OLYMPIC DELEGATION

While Yao was honored to carry the flag, he was focused on proving that China could compete in the international game.

His experiences with the NBA would be valuable to the Chinese team. Yao and Coach Del Harris, who was an assistant coach with the Dallas Mavericks, brought a toughness to the Chinese team that had been lacking in previous years.

"We're going to have a muscled-up team that's going to be more physical than any Chinese team before," Harris said.

Yao had a simpler view of what was needed. "It's going to be a very tough competition," he said. "We have to work hard because other teams are working hard."

China's first 2004 Olympic game was on August 15 against Spain. The Spanish team was led by Pau Gasol, who also played with the NBA's Memphis Grizzlies. Early on, China's high hopes seemed justified as Yao led the team to a 16–13 lead. At one point, Yao accidentally knocked Gasol in the face and caused him to miss several minutes. But Spain was a much more experienced team, and eventually their experience showed. Gasol and Spain routed the Chinese team. Yao was frustrated. He stormed toward China's bench, waving his arms and shouting at his teammates. This was rare behavior for Yao and the type of antics almost never seen in Chinese sports. Yao fouled out of the game with about 4 minutes to play, but the contest was over long before that. The 83–58 defeat was an embarrassment to Yao, who displayed uncharacteristic frustration after the game.

"I feel so disappointed," he said. "I lost all my hopes for this team. I didn't expect to play so bad. I am thinking of retiring from the national team. Not now, but soon I will."

China rebounded two days later with a 69–62 win over New Zealand. A very angry Yao was almost unstoppable in the game. He scored 39 points, including 21 in the third quarter alone. In the third game, however, Argentina crushed the Chinese 82–57 (Yao scored 15 points). Then Italy dominated the Chinese team, playing great team defense and holding Yao to only 9 points. Italy beat China 89–52. Things weren't looking good for China to advance to the elimination (medal) round. They weren't just losing, they were getting blown out. But China still had a chance to make the medal round if Yao and his teammates could win their final game.

The bad news was that their opponent was Serbia-Montenegro, the defending world champions, who were also fighting for a spot in the medal round. Serbia-Montenegro was loaded with talent, including five NBA players. Many fans expected Yao and his teammates to face another blow-out. But Yao wouldn't go away quietly. He was tough in the paint, scoring and pulling down rebounds. With 7 minutes to play, China trailed by 7 points. The Chinese clamped down on defense, smothering the Serbian team, especially in the paint. Meanwhile, they slowly worked their way back. With

45 seconds to play, Yao made two free throws to tie the game 63–63. He made two more free throws 17 seconds later to give China the lead. Then, with time running out, he defended a desperation 3-point attempt by a Serbian player and secured the shocking win. Yao and the Chinese team had done it! They stormed onto the court to celebrate one of the biggest wins in the history of Chinese basketball. They were headed to the medal round.

"Today is indeed a day of great joy for us," Yao said. "Coach Harris has taught us the lesson of life. You should never give up no matter the circumstances."

A HAIRY SITUATION

Yao was so sure that China would do well at the 2004 Olympics that he vowed not to shave for six months if the team failed to make the quarterfinals (final eight). "I hope we will have the chance to visit all the ancient monuments of Athens and experience the Olympic tradition of this unique country," he said. "But first of all we have to qualify for the next round, for the quarterfinals. If we don't, I won't shave for six months as punishment."

It was as far as China would go. They faced undefeated Lithuania in the quarterfinals. Yao did his part, scoring 29 points and pulling down 11 rebounds. But Lithuania was just too good and won the game 95–75. China played one last game, the seventh-place game, against Spain. Once again they lost, 92–76 (Yao scored 14 points). In total, the team finished just 2–5 at the Olympics.

Yao needed to shift his focus again and look ahead to the regular season. Rockets fans were understandably excited. With McGrady in the mix, there was no telling how good Houston might be.

The Houston Rockets and the Sacramento Kings traveled to Shanghai in October 2004 to play two preseason games. They were the first NBA games played in China. The teams split the games, with Yao's Rockets winning the opener 88–86, then losing the second game 91–89.

At first, however, the new combination of players struggled. In early December, their record was a disappointing 6–11. Yao was playing better than ever, though, and soon the Rockets turned the season around. On December 20, Yao and McGrady teamed up to give Houston one of its most impressive wins of the year. Yao scored 40 points and McGrady added 34 in a 114–102 win over the Toronto Raptors.

"This team is very different from last season's and Tracy and I have only really played together for a few months," Yao wrote in an online journal. "In many ways we are still very much getting to know each other on the court, and that takes time. I am excited about where this team is headed though and I believe that things are starting to really gel now."

An eight-game winning streak for the Rockets in late January and early February pushed their record to 32–21. Once again, Yao was selected to start in the All-Star Game alongside McGrady. In fact, he set an NBA record with the most votes ever received, with 2,558,278, many of the votes coming from China. In limited playing time, Yao scored 11 points and snagged 8 rebounds in the West's 125–115 loss.

Yao played great down the stretch as the Rockets fought to secure a good playoff spot. On March 11, Yao's 27 points and 22 rebounds helped the Rockets defeat the Phoenix Suns 127–107.

The Rockets got hot again at the end of the season, winning their final seven games to earn the number-five seed in the Western Conference playoffs. The highlight of the streak for Yao was a 28-point, 4-block performance in a 100–92 victory over the Memphis Grizzlies.

The Rockets squared off with one of their home-state rivals, the Dallas Mavericks, in the first round of the playoffs. Dallas, led by forward Dirk Nowitzki, was heavily favored in the series. But during Game 1, played in Dallas, the Mavericks couldn't stop McGrady, whose 34 points led the Rockets to a surprising win. Yao didn't play particularly well in the game. He scored only 11 points on 3–8 shooting from the field.

Yao made his presence felt in Game 2, however. He was almost unstoppable, draining shot after shot. But with a little more than a minute to go, the game was tied 109–109. McGrady had the ball. He quickly drove into the lane, drawing Dallas defenders. Then he slipped the ball over to Yao, who jammed it home for a 2-point lead. The basket gave Yao a game-high 33 points on 13–14 shooting.

During a time-out, McGrady and Yao hatched a plan. If Dallas scored on the following possession, they'd be ready with a surprise of their own. Sure enough, Nowitzki made a game-tying jump shot with 10 seconds left. Almost everyone in the building expected the Rockets to take a time-out. Even most of the Houston players expected it. But Yao and McGrady had a different idea. McGrady quickly darted up the court with the ball. There, Yao was ready to do his part. He got his big body between McGrady and the Dallas defender, a move called a screen. Left open, McGrady drained a long 2-point basket. The

Rockets had won the game 113–111 and had taken a command-ing 2–0 lead in the series!

"We shocked [Dallas] a little bit by not calling time-out," McGrady said. "My teammates didn't even know. The only peo-ple who knew were me and Yao. I saw them scrambling on the defensive end. We caught them off guard pretty good."

Yao was pleased with the win and optimistic about Houston's chances to advance. "We can go very far this year, if we keep it up," he told reporters.

"I don't want to put that pressure on [Yao], but he can be an outstanding player in this league. He can become a dominant force in this league if he continues to play the way he played last night.**"**
—TRACY MCGRADY AFTER YAO'S 33-POINT PERFORMANCE
IN GAME 2 AGAINST THE MAVERICKS

The Rockets seemed to be firmly in control of the series, which moved to Houston for Game 3. The Rocket fans were pumped up, and the team gave them even more reason to cheer by building an 88–80 lead early in the fourth quarter. Houston just had to hold on to take a 3–0 lead in the series. But from that moment, everything fell apart. Dallas made one shot after another, while Houston seemed unable to do anything right. The stunned Houston crowd watched as Dallas scored the next 20 points and went on to win the game, 106–100.

Game 4 was another heartbreak for the Rockets. Yao scored 20 points on 6–7 shooting and McGrady had 36 points, but it wasn't enough. Dallas pulled out another close game, 97–93, to tie the series at two games each.

Yao tried to be positive after the loss, reminding reporters that the series was still tied. "We're just starting over, like it's 0–0."

McGrady, however, appeared more frustrated. A big part of his frustration stemmed from the fact that Yao had gotten only 7 shots in the game. "Somehow, some way, we got to get the guy the ball," he said. "He has to take more than seven or eight shots. If he doesn't produce and doesn't get the ball, regardless of what I do, we don't win."

McGrady got his wish. In Game 5 in Dallas, Yao made 10 of 13 shots from the field for a game-high 30 points. But foul trouble forced him to sit for long stretches of the second half, and once again Dallas won a tight game, 103–100.

The Rockets won Game 6, 101–83, despite getting just 8 points from Yao. The series was tied 3–3. The winner of Game 7 would advance to the second round. The Dallas crowd was filled with excitement, and both teams were pumped for the game. But the Rockets came out flat. Dallas jumped out to a big lead while Houston was visibly frustrated. Dallas led by 12 after the first quarter and 15 at the half. And it only got worse in the second half. By the time the final buzzer sounded, the Mavericks had a 116–76 victory. The 40-point win marked the largest Game 7 margin in history.

CONSPIRACY THEORY

During the 2005 playoff series against Dallas, Houston coach Jeff Van Gundy claimed that the officials were unfairly targeting Yao for foul calls. "I believe what I believe," Van Gundy said. "I've seen what I've seen." The coach was fined $100,000 for his statements—the largest fine on a coach in league history. Yao stood beside his coach and even offered to pay half of the fine.

In 2008, a former official under investigation for gambling on NBA games told investigators that officials had indeed singled out Yao. The NBA denied the accusation.

"We cracked in every way," Van Gundy said. "It was really not befitting how we played and conducted ourselves this year. . . . The way it ended . . . [shows] how very, very far we have to go."

Yao Ming poses with his parents, Fang Feng Di *(center)* and Yao Zhi Yuan *(left)*, in China after being made eligible for the 2002 NBA draft.

Yao played for the Shanghai Sharks from 1997 to 2002. He is seen here in 2002.

Yao scores his first 2-point shot for the Houston Rockets over San Antonio Spurs star David Robinson on October 23, 2002.

Rockets head coach Jeff Van Gundy gives Yao some words of advice during a 2005 playoff game.

Yao goes up against legendary center Shaquille O'Neal in a 2006 game against the Miami Heat.

Rockets trainers check on Yao after he collapses with an injury in 2006. He later found out he had broken a bone in his knee.

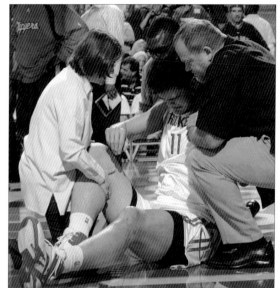

Yao and his wife, Ye Li, pose for a wedding portrait in Hangzhou, China, the week of their 2007 wedding.

Yao and earthquake survivor Lin Hao lead the Chinese athletes into the national stadium, nicknamed the Bird's Nest, during the opening ceremony for the 2008 Olympic Games in Beijing.

Yao and his teammates on the Chinese national team celebrate a win over Germany during the preliminary round at the 2008 Olympics.

© FILIPPO MONTEFORTE/AFP/Getty Images

© Layne Murdoch/NBAE/Getty Images

Tracy McGrady and Yao talk on the bench during a 2008 game. The two star players are the backbone of the Houston Rockets team.

With a 2004–2005 regular-season scoring average of 18.3, Yao was clearly one of the better centers in the NBA. But he hadn't done much to improve on his first two seasons. Was Yao destined to become a truly dominant NBA center? Or was this as good as Rockets fans could ever expect him to be? Some fans suggested that he needed to add strength. But others believed that all Yao really needed was something he hadn't had in almost three years—a rest.

Chapter Seven

A Force on the Court

Yao had played three full seasons in the NBA, which meant that he had just one year left on his contract. The Rockets didn't want to risk letting his contract expire after the season. So before the 2005–2006 season, they gave him a five-year extension worth $75 million.

"This is an exciting time for the Rockets," owner Leslie Alexander said. "Yao is going to be a part of the Rockets for a long time. I feel he'll become one of the great players in NBA history. He's got the size, intelligence, youth, and quickness to be a phenomenal, forceful player in the league.

"It's as important as anything I've ever done as owner. To have the next great big man of the NBA, it's very important for the team and the city."

Yao was just as pleased. "I'm thankful for Mr. Alexander's trust and giving me the opportunity to play in Houston," he told reporters. "I can put more energy into next season and future seasons now that the [contract] matter has been put aside. This was something in my mind, and my heart is always in Houston."

❝*It was not difficult [to re-sign] because I love Houston and I have very good teammates. I think our team is getting stronger. Everything is getting comfortable for me.*❞
—YAO ON HIS CONTRACT EXTENSION

Understandably, the Rockets entered the 2005–2006 season with high expectations. The addition of McGrady had lifted the team to new heights the previous season. With Yao and McGrady back, Rockets fans had every reason to look forward to another winning year. But injuries quickly derailed the season. McGrady missed eight of the team's first fourteen games with injuries. Yao did all he could to pick up the slack, but the team missed McGrady's offensive punch. The Rockets started with a 3–11 record, which was not a promising beginning.

"[With McGrady's injury], teams can double-team me without any trouble," said a frustrated Yao. "They don't have to worry about anyone else scoring."

When McGrady returned, the Rockets won six of eight games. But by then, Yao was having injury problems of his own. The big toe on his left foot was hurting him. By late December, the pain forced him to sit out. Doctors diagnosed him with a condition called osteomyelitis, which is a type of bone infection. Yao needed surgery to correct the problem, forcing him to miss the team's next twenty-one games. Just as they had with McGrady out, the Rockets struggled badly without Yao, going just 6–15 during that stretch.

In his second game back on the court, Yao showed why he was such a big part of the team. He scored 21 points and grabbed 13 rebounds in an 86–84 victory over the Milwaukee Bucks.

"I think I'm still not in great shape now because it's only been two games," Yao said after the win. "We struggled scoring in the fourth quarter and let them back in the game. But we played pretty good defense the last couple of minutes."

The win over Milwaukee sparked the Rockets' best stretch of basketball that season. They won fourteen of their next eighteen games to improve their season mark to 29–33 and surge back into the playoff race. Yao was named the Western Conference Player of the Week for the week of February 21, when he averaged 26.7 points and 15.7 rebounds. He was also named a starter for the All-Star Game, once again as the leading vote-getter. (He scored 15 points in the West's 122–121 loss.)

The Rockets capped their hot streak with a 103–99 victory over Indiana on March 8. Yao was completely dominant in the game. He scored 38 points, claimed 10 rebounds, and blocked 5 Indiana shots. Better yet, it was his third-straight game scoring 30 or more points.

❝I know my job. I know what the team needs me to do. I need to score, rebound, guard people. I know who I am and I know what I need to do.**❞**

—YAO AFTER SCORING 38 POINTS
AGAINST THE PACERS ON MARCH 8, 2006

"The big fella, he's really putting us on his back," said Rockets guard Rafer Alston. But all the news wasn't good. McGrady had been struggling with back problems again, and the Indiana game would be his last of the year. Just when the Rockets seemed to be on their way to the top, their best player was out.

Yao did all he could to carry the team. The Rockets lost the first three games without McGrady, even though Yao scored 25, 26, and 36 points. The losses set the tone for the rest of the season. After the All-Star break, Yao averaged 25.7 points and 11.6 rebounds per game. But with McGrady out, he just didn't have the supporting cast he needed. The Rockets won only five of their final twenty games.

On April 10, with just five games left in the season, the Rockets were playing the Utah Jazz. Late in the first quarter, Utah's Mehmet Okur accidentally kicked the side of Yao's foot. Yao was in a lot of pain, but he tried to keep playing. He even made a 3-point play before finally limping to the bench.

Doctors gave Yao the bad news. His left foot was broken. After the game, Yao tried to look on the bright side. "Maybe it's the best thing for me and when I come back I'll be stronger," he told reporters.

Yao missed Houston's final four games and twenty-five games total for the year. But in the games he did play, he'd been better than ever. He averaged 22.3 points per game, an impressive improvement of more than 5 points per game over his average in the previous season. He also averaged 10.2 rebounds per game. Yao was clearly a player on the rise. He just needed to stay healthy.

In 2005–2006, Yao and McGrady played only thirty-one games together. In those games, the Rockets went 21–10. In the remaining games, the team went 13–38.

Yao was off the hard court for several months, but that didn't mean he was out of the headlines, especially in China. He did something that is rare among Chinese celebrities by standing up against a practice of his own culture. In an August press conference in Beijing, China, Yao denounced the eating of shark fin soup, a Chinese delicacy. Yao argued that the Chinese should stop the practice of catching endangered sharks and sawing off their fins.

"Endangered species are our friends," Yao told reporters. He later added, "Putting our ecosystem in great peril is certainly not a part of Chinese culture that I know. How do you maintain this so-called tradition when one day there is no shark to be [caught]?"

While in China, Yao was busy letting his broken foot heal. He wanted to be ready for the 2006 World Championships in Japan. Many experts assumed he would miss the games, but to the surprise of many, he was ready to go when the tournament started in August.

The Chinese team started out slowly in the preliminary round. They lost their opening game to Italy 84–69, despite 30 points from Yao. Then they faced the powerful U.S. team. The Americans structured their entire defense around stopping Yao.

"We knew that they wanted Yao to be a big factor," said U.S. forward Antawn Jamison. "So we wanted to take him out and make them take difficult shots."

The U.S. team did exactly that. Their defense swarmed around Yao, while the powerful American offense jumped out to a 10-point lead within the opening minutes. The U.S. team never looked back, building that lead as high as 36 points.

Despite the extra defensive attention, Yao managed to play well, scoring 21 points. But the American team just had too much firepower. They gave China its second straight loss, 121–90.

❝It is a little bit different from playing Yao in international ball than NBA ball. Yao is the main focus for the Chinese team. Playing with him in America, he has Tracy McGrady on his team, so Yao kind of gets some rest.❞

—U.S. FORWARD DWIGHT HOWARD ON PLAYING YAO IN THE 2006 WORLD CHAMPIONSHIPS

China hoped to score a win against Puerto Rico in the third game. They started out well with Yao scoring 29. But with 4:40 to play, Yao fouled out of the game. China wasn't the same without him and lost 90–87 in overtime. The Chinese team was 0–3. To have any chance to advance to the final round, they'd have to win both of their remaining games in preliminary play.

Number Three?

Yao is a hero in China, but in 2006, his jersey wasn't at the top of China's sales charts. According to the NBA, McGrady's was the highest-selling jersey in China. Guard Allen Iverson's was second. Yao's number-11 jersey came in third place.

China started with a 100–83 comeback win over Senegal, which set up a must-win contest with Slovenia. Slovenia looked like the better team early in the game, taking a 46–38 lead into halftime. But Yao and the Chinese team didn't give up. Early in the fourth quarter, Yao made a 3-point play to finally give China the lead. The game remained close down the stretch. It was tied 75–75 when Slovenia scored with just 6 seconds remaining. Chinese guard Wang Shipeng took the ball and sprinted down the court. He launched a three-pointer as time ran out and *swish*! The shot gave China a thrilling 78–77 win and a trip to the knockout round.

"This was so exciting," Yao said after the game. "So dramatic. I just gave someone $500 to go buy souvenirs. I want to remember this."

The game would be China's last highlight of the tournament. They were no match for Greece, their opponent in the first knockout round. Greece took the stop-Yao defense to a new extreme, often devoting two or even three defenders to him. The strategy worked. Yao scored a tournament-low 10 points, and Greece breezed to a 95–64 blowout.

Yao finished as the tournament's leading scorer, averaging 25.3 points per game. But he was disappointed with the result. "I cannot say it was a great success for our team," he said. "All we did was to make our lowest goal. We made it out of the first round and reached the first elimination game. Then we were eliminated."

Chapter Eight

A Return to the Playoffs

Expectations for the Rockets were high entering the 2006–2007 season. The team had worked hard during the off-season to improve the supporting cast, adding key players such as Shane Battier and Bonzi Wells. The hope was that a stronger roster from top to bottom would take some of the pressure off Yao and McGrady.

"We never put together this much new talent in one year since I've owned the team," said Leslie Alexander. "I think we can do very well."

Yao was a little more reserved in his optimism. He was concerned about learning to play alongside so many new players. "I worry about chemistry," he said. "We have ten new guys. Chemistry may [present] some problems.... We need better communication to pass through those times. That's very important for us."

Yao started the season on fire. In the second game, he scored 36 points in a 107–76 blowout of Dallas. He made 12 of 16 shots from the field and also drained all 12 free throws he attempted.

"When we double-teamed him, triple-teamed him, or single-covered him, he would still score," said Dallas coach Avery Johnson. "He was playing like we were not out there on the floor."

❝I'd call [Yao] the hardest-working player in the league. He's a tremendous ambassador for his country, the game, and really how you want to conduct yourself. If you notice, most of his quotes are team oriented. He doesn't refer to himself in the third person, he hasn't given himself a nickname. It's really refreshing.❞

—JEFF VAN GUNDY

Yao's great play continued throughout the early part of the season. He wasn't just playing well, he was utterly dominating the competition. Finally, everything seemed to be coming together for the twenty-six-year-old. Yao continued to shine even against the strongest competition. On November 12, he scored 34 points and grabbed 14 rebounds in a 94–72 win over

Shaq and the Miami Heat. The win lifted the Rockets to 5–2 for the young season.

"My only chance against Shaq is to keep him on the run," Yao said. "Shaq is much stronger and bigger than me. My only chance of beating him is to keep running and running against him. Every time I score on him I was happy like a kid, like a kid getting candy on Halloween because it's really too hard to score on him, too hard. He's just great."

Yao's fantastic play was getting notice all around the league. He'd always been one of the NBA's most popular players, but his play was also making him one of its best. It didn't take long before experts started pointing to Yao as a potential league MVP candidate. In November, he averaged 25.7 points and a league-high 13.6 rebounds. He shot better than 57 percent from the field and was named the Western Conference Player of the Month. Even more impressive, Yao had the Rockets winning even with McGrady missing a lot of time due to injury.

One of Yao's most memorable games came December 9 against the Washington Wizards. Through three quarters, Yao had scored 15 points and helped Houston build a slim lead. Washington used a combination of four different centers to try to slow down the big man, but none of them could contend with Yao.

Yao got stronger and stronger as the game went on. By the fourth quarter, he was all but unstoppable. He scored Houston's first 12 points of the quarter, and went on to net a total of 23 (giving him 38 for the game). The most thrilling shot of the night was Yao's last. The Rockets had the ball and were clinging to a 1-point lead with less than 15 seconds to go. Yao took a pass from Battier and made his move on defender Calvin Booth. He quickly turned, jumped, and released a hook shot that swished through the net to extend the lead to 3 points. The basket helped secure a 114–109 win and a record of 14–6 for the year.

"I don't think anybody has an answer [on how to defend Yao]," said Washington head coach Eddie Jordan. "You have to do the best you can. . . . The guy has an arsenal that I haven't seen before."

Yao's teammates were coming to expect those kinds of performances from their center. In his next five games, Yao scored 26, 38, 35, 32, and 34 points. He seemed almost unstoppable on both ends of the court. His offense was better than ever, while his defense remained outstanding.

But on December 23, everything changed. Six minutes into a game against the Los Angeles Clippers, Yao and the Rockets were playing defense. Clipper forward Tim Thomas drove the ball into the lane. Yao moved to block the shot. Houston's

Chuck Hayes also moved in to defend the play. Thomas and Hayes crashed into each other, and they both fell into Yao. As Yao crashed to the floor, he grabbed his right leg and shouted in pain. He had to be carried off the court.

"I didn't even know what happened," Hayes said. "I heard somebody yelling and turned around, and it was Yao. I saw he wasn't getting up and knew it was serious."

The bad news came later that night. Yao had fractured his right tibia, a bone in the lower leg, near his knee. His doctors said he'd be out of action for at least six weeks.

"I feel badly for Yao," Van Gundy said. "If ever there was an athlete who didn't deserve all the bad breaks he's gotten over the last two years with injuries [it's Yao]. He works hard and is in great shape, so I feel badly for him."

❝Six weeks minimum. That means it could be more. That's our guy. You're talking about a guy on an MVP pace, that's been carrying this team the past two seasons. To hear that, it hurts. When he hit the ground, I was looking at him. You can tell sometimes the way a player reacts. He was yelling and screaming and I was hoping that it wasn't the worst.❞

—ROCKETS GUARD RAFER ALSTON ON YAO'S BROKEN KNEE

Six weeks wasn't long enough for Yao to heal fully. He missed all of January and February, a total of 32 games. Finally, in early March, he was ready to return to a Rockets team that badly needed him. Houston had actually managed a winning record in Yao's absence, but even with a mark of 36–23, the team was in the thick of a tough Western Conference playoff race.

Yao stepped onto the court on March 5 in Cleveland wearing a knee brace. It was a reminder that he still had to be careful. The leg was well enough to play on, but it still wasn't completely healed.

"The knee is very important for a basketball player and I don't know if it's going to bother me in a live game," Yao said before his first game back. "Practice and a game are still different."

Yao looked rusty in his return. He made just 5 of 15 shots in a 91–85 loss. He and the Rockets got a scare late in the game. With a minute to play, Houston was trailing by 4 points. Yao grabbed an offensive rebound and moved toward the basket. But Cleveland center Zydrunas Ilgauskas stepped in front of Yao, causing him to crash to the ground and lose the ball. Luckily, Yao managed not to fall on his knee, though he and his teammates were upset that no foul was called.

After the game, Yao iced his knee and told reporters that he hadn't felt like himself on the court. "In the second quarter, third quarter, I was almost like a high school player," he said. "Sometimes, Cleveland would just steal the ball from my hand.

"I can't wait for my next game," he added. It didn't take Yao long to start feeling confident again. On March 9, he scored 24 points and grabbed 13 rebounds in a 112–91 win over the New Jersey Nets. Two nights later, he poured in 37 points in a win over the Magic. With such great numbers, one might think Yao was back up to speed, but that wasn't the case. The knee was still bothering him.

"It's getting better every day," he said. "But my turnovers are still too high and my rebounds are still too low. I don't know how long it will be before I make it all the way back. I don't have experience with this kind of injury, so I don't know how long to say."

With both Yao and McGrady in the lineup, the Rockets were playing great. From March 5 to March 30, they went 11–3 to secure a playoff spot. Yao capped the hot streak with a season-high 39 points in a 107–104 win over the Lakers.

 Yao was named to the 2006–2007 All-NBA Second Team.

By season's end, the Rockets had an impressive record of 52–30, fourth best in the Western Conference. In the playoffs, they would face off with the Utah Jazz, which had finished the year just a game behind, at 51–31. It promised to be a tough, physical, evenly matched series. The Jazz were built around a stifling defense. That defense would do all it could to make sure Yao, who had averaged a career-high 25 points per game during the season, wouldn't get any easy baskets.

Yao went into the series with more intensity than ever. Usually, he liked to relax before a big game. He often played video games to stay loose. But before the Utah series, he devoted himself to studying the scouting reports on the Jazz. He told one reporter that he was waking up in the middle of the night thinking about the Jazz and how they might play.

The series opened on April 21 in Houston. The Jazz jumped out to a 9-point lead at halftime, and the Rockets often looked nervous. McGrady was especially shaky in the first half, so the Rockets went to Yao again and again. He dominated early, scoring 6 of Houston's first 8 points.

But Utah didn't make it easy on Yao, playing him very physically. The Jazz sent Yao to the free-throw stripe fourteen times in the game (Yao made 12 of the 14 shots). Finally, in the second half, McGrady caught fire, and the Rockets surged to a lead. Houston outscored Utah 26–11 in the third quarter and never looked back. Yao scored a game-high 28 points in the 84–75 win.

Game 2 was much like the first. Utah jumped out to a 9-point lead after one quarter, then the Rockets fought back to take the lead. Once again, the Jazz weren't afraid to foul Yao, and once again, the big man made them pay by going 9–9 from the free-throw line. Yao scored 27 points and McGrady had 31 as the Rockets took a commanding 2–0 lead in the series. Things were looking great for Houston, but the Rockets knew that the next two games would be in Utah. Could they keep winning on the road?

66*Trying to defend [Yao] is a monumental task.*99
—UTAH JAZZ COACH JERRY SLOAN

"[The Jazz] play very physical and they're not afraid to foul. I don't remember any of their players having foul trouble. But I felt like I was fouled many times," Yao said. "They still keep playing very aggressively. They always go very aggressive against us on the defensive side, trying to push us away from the paint, away from the basket."

That philosophy worked for Utah in Game 3. They continued to play Yao very physically. This time, despite Yao knocking down 14 of 16 free throws, Utah's rough style seemed to throw the Rockets off their game. The Rockets couldn't seem to do anything right on the offensive end. In the third quarter, they managed just 10 points as a team. By game's end, a frustrated Rockets team walked off the court with an 81–67 loss. Forward Shane Battier had added 11 points to Yao's 26 and McGrady's 24, while Alston netted 6. Those four players had scored all of the team's points! It is very unusual for only four players on a team to score during a game.

The news for Rockets fans didn't get any better in the next game. Yao led the team with 20 points, but once again, Utah's defense dominated. By the fourth quarter, Yao was visibly frustrated. Utah's Mehmet Okur was defending him and had been playing rough with Yao throughout the series, constantly trying to swat the ball away from the Houston center. Yao had finally had enough, and he threw his elbow into Okur's chin. The whistle blew. An offensive foul was called on Yao. That play summed up Houston's frustration over a 98–85 loss. The series was tied at two games each.

The series returned to Houston for Game 5. The change of scenery was welcome for Yao and his teammates. The game was tight through three quarters. In the fourth quarter, Yao and McGrady took over. Yao made two free throws with 11 seconds left to seal a 96–92 victory and to reclaim control of the series.

With a 3–2 lead, the Rockets would have two chances to get a win and advance to the second round.

CHARITABLE YAO

Yao has always been eager to give back. He supports charities both in China and the United States. Some of the causes he has taken up include working for AIDS prevention and care, helping to rebuild New Orleans after Hurricane Katrina, and spreading basketball in China and around the world. In 2007, he and Phoenix's Steve Nash put on a basketball game to benefit a variety of charities, including one that helps develop education in poor parts of China. In 2008, Yao started the Yao Ming Foundation to help rebuild schools after a terrible earthquake struck his homeland. Yao announced that he would donate $2 million of his own money to the cause.

The series moved back to Utah for Game 6, and once again the Jazz dominated on their home court, 94–82. Yao scored 25 points in the loss, but that didn't tell the whole story. He struggled with ball control, turning over the ball eight times. He was making silly mistakes at critical moments. He wasn't playing smart basketball, and his poor play was hurting his team.

"It's disappointing," Van Gundy said of Yao's mistakes. "He's proven before that he can play efficient basketball and not turn it over. He's just not done it in this series."

The series came down to a winner-takes-all Game 7, played in Houston. Through the first six games of the series, the home team had won every time. Could the Rockets continue that trend and advance to the second round? The Jazz jumped out early and built a 10-point lead at halftime, but the Rockets fought back in the second half.

With just about a minute left in the game, Houston trailed by 4 points. Yao got the ball down low. Instead of settling for a jump shot, he made a strong move toward the basket, jumping toward the rim to dunk the ball. The Utah defender hacked Yao's arm and fouled him. Yao stepped to the free-throw line and calmly sank both shots, pulling the Rockets to within 2 points. The Houston crowd was going wild.

But 2 points was as close as the Rockets would get. The Jazz held on for a 103–99 victory. Once again, Yao and his teammates were playoff losers. And once again, they'd blown a 2–0 series lead.

Yao, who scored 29 points in the loss, was crushed. After the game, he sat in the locker room, staring at the floor. "I feel like I want to cry," he told reporters. "I know everyone says that tomorrow is a new day and that I'll have a long career, but in the last two weeks we've gone from up 2–0 all the way to 3–4, and it's all over for our season. That's very frustrating.

"There's no way to get past this," Yao added. "We have to go through it. Whatever people say, we have to take it. If we hurt, we hurt. You know what? There are no shortcuts. You have to put your passion into the summer workouts and prepare for next season. The only way to get through is [when] you get your next chance, don't let it pass."

Chapter Nine

Looking toward Beijing

Between his injury and the loss to the Jazz in the playoffs, the 2006–2007 season had been a disappointment for Yao. But soon he was looking forward to an exciting year, and it wasn't all about basketball. On August 6, 2007, Yao and his longtime girlfriend, Ye Li, were married in a private ceremony in Shanghai. After the wedding, the couple headed to Beijing, where the one-year countdown had begun to another event Yao was eagerly anticipating: the 2008 Summer Olympics.

Yao and Ye Li's wedding reportedly cost more than $1 million yuan (about $130,000). It was held at the fancy Shangri-La Hotel in Shanghai. After the ceremony, the couple and their guests went on a cruise along the Huangpu River.

But before Yao could think ahead to the Olympics, he had a job to do. He had yet to win a playoff series in the NBA, and he started the 2007–2008 season focused on doing just that. The collapse to Utah in the playoffs had cost Van Gundy his job, so the new season brought a new coach, Rick Adelman. Adelman had previously coached for Sacramento, Golden State, and Portland. He was best known for his approach to offense, while Van Gundy had focused on defense.

In the preseason, Yao was concerned with Adelman's new offensive approach. He wasn't sure how he fit into the fast-paced system. He was used to a slower, more methodical approach to offense. In Adelman's offense, Yao spent less time in the low post (the area right in front of the basket), which was his comfort zone.

An old friend returned to the Rockets in the 2007–2008 season. Steve Francis signed with his old team. Francis, however, suffered a season-ending knee injury after playing in just ten games with the team.

Yao adjusted and scored 25 points in the opening-night win over the Lakers. He also helped Houston to win six of its first seven games. The hot start was quickly followed by a six-game losing streak as the Rockets struggled to find their identity in the early months of the season. Yao wasn't scoring as consistently as he had in the previous season. He'd score 31 points one night and 10 the next.

The low point for the Rockets came in early January. After a loss to the Boston Celtics, their record stood at 15–17. McGrady was frequently out with knee problems, and although the season wasn't even half over, the team's playoff hopes didn't seem bright. But on January 4, all of that turned around in Orlando. Yao's aggressive play caused the Orlando Magic's best player, center Dwight Howard, to foul out, and the Rockets took advantage with a 96–94 win.

YAO, MEET YI

In 2007, another Chinese player, Yi Jianlian, joined the NBA. The Milwaukee Bucks made Yi the sixth-overall pick of the 2007 draft. In his rookie season, Yi averaged 8.6 points per game. After the Bucks played the Rockets, Yao told reporters that Yi would someday be the better player of the two. Yi was traded to the New Jersey Nets before the 2008–2009 season.

From that point, the Rockets were red hot. They won their next four games. On January 27, Yao had to sit out of a game because he was sick. The Rockets lost to the Jazz 97–89. It would be their last loss for a long time.

Yao was back on the court two nights later. He scored 36 points and grabbed 19 rebounds in a 111–107 victory over Golden State. The Rockets won their next three games, all on the road. Then they destroyed Cleveland, one of the league's best teams, 92–77.

The wins kept coming: eight games in a row by the All-Star break. (Yao was once again the Western Conference's starting center in the All-Star Game.) The streak grew to ten games with a 112–100 win over Miami on February 21. Yao dropped 28 points on the New Orleans Hornets on February 22 to extend the streak to eleven games. It was also Houston's tenth-straight road victory.

"We talked about making a statement," said Adelman. "We feel we're playing as well as anybody in the league right now and we want to show that we can continue to do that by playing the best teams and getting the win."

The Rockets hosted the Bulls on February 26, looking to extend the streak to twelve games. Yao didn't play his best in the game, scoring just 12 points. Pain in his left foot was partly to blame. But Yao's troubles didn't slow down the Rockets. They won the game 110–97 and kept the winning streak alive.

The next day, all the good feelings went away. Doctors had examined Yao's foot and found that he had fractured a bone. It was not good news. Yao's season was over. The twenty-seven-year-old was crushed.

Yao's teammates shared his disappointment. "When Coach tells everybody I am out for the season, everybody is like quiet," Yao said, discussing the team's reaction to the bad news. "That kind of quietness makes me feel kind of scared, it was quiet like nobody was there and you just feel alone."

But the bad news didn't end there. Doctors doubted that Yao's foot would heal in time for him to play for China in the Summer Olympics. Yao had been looking forward to playing for his nation's fans for years. "If I cannot play in the Olympics for my country this time, it will be the biggest loss in my career to right now," he said.

After surgery, Yao watched his teammates continue in their quest for a playoff spot. They didn't let the loss of Yao get them down. They kept on winning, extending their streak to fifteen games, then to twenty. Their 104–92 victory over the Lakers on March 16 pushed the streak to twenty-two games, the second longest in NBA history. The streak finally ended two nights later in a game against Boston, but the Rockets had already all but claimed a playoff spot. They finished the season at 55–27 and once again squared off with the Utah Jazz in the playoffs.

Without Yao in the middle, however, the Rockets had no chance against the Jazz. They lost the first two games at home and never recovered. Utah won the series four games to two, making the Rockets first-round losers once again.

According to the 2008 *Sports Illustrated* International 20, Yao's yearly earnings of more than $31 million ranked him eighth in the world among non-American athletes. Soccer star David Beckham topped the international list at more than $48 million, while Tiger Woods was number one among American athletes with a whopping $128 million.

Yao continued to focus on getting healthy for the Olympics. The Rockets didn't want him to compete. They worried that if he came back too soon, he could make the injured foot even worse. But Yao was determined. He was going to play in front of his home fans.

The Olympics were a big deal for the Chinese. The nation badly wanted to make a good impression on the international community. China wanted to show that it was a fully modern, powerful nation. And having Yao as one of the faces of the nation would be a big part of that. Yao was once again China's flag bearer in the opening ceremonies. The crowd of more than 90,000 roared as Yao led the Chinese athletes onto the field of Beijing's National Stadium. Yao walked with Lin Hao, a nine-year-old boy who had rescued two of his classmates after the terrible earthquake in China earlier in the year.

A Letter from Yao

After his injury, Yao sent a letter to his fans through the Chinese newspapers, assuring them that he would do all he could to play in the Olympics. Here is some of what he wrote:

> My injury has made many of you worried and you expressed your concern and sympathy in many ways. You have always supported me and encouraged me at the lowest point of my career. And now I want to say thank you for your care and support. . . . The surgery was very successful and I'll start physical recovery very soon. I'll do whatever I can to overcome the difficulty and play for China in Olympics and be in my best form.

But even more exciting for Chinese fans was the news that Yao was ready to play. His foot was healed, he insisted, and he wasn't about to miss out on the action. Playing to win was a tall task, though. With or without Yao, few experts believed China would get very far in the games. The team still hadn't caught up to Western-style basketball. Some said that Yao had no business playing on a foot that couldn't possibly be fully healed. He was risking his entire career, they said, and he didn't even have a realistic shot at a medal.

These rulings didn't matter to Yao. His mind was made up. He was on the court on August 10 for China's opening game against the United States. China kept the game close for the first 15 minutes before the powerful U.S. team pulled away. Even after the outcome was long decided, Yao was on the court, battling for every rebound and doing everything he could to compete. The United States won the game 101–70. But for many who watched the action, the sight of Yao giving his all before his home fans, even though he was clearly still hobbled and in pain from his injury, made a lasting impression.

Just being able to play was a victory for Yao. "This game was a treasure, and it will be for the rest of my life," he said.

"Yao is an unbelievable person," U.S. guard Chris Paul said. "This wasn't just a basketball game for the people here, and Yao understood that."

China was the underdog again for its second game, against Spain, the world champions. But Yao and his teammates came out on fire, feeding off the crowd. They took a 46–37 lead into halftime and extended that to 61–47 entering the fourth quarter. But then the team stumbled. Spain, led by forward Pau Gasol, stormed back to tie the game and send it into overtime. In the overtime, Yao fouled out, and Gasol and Spain took over. The final score of 85–75 didn't really tell the story of how close the game was.

There was no moral victory for Yao this time. "We had so many chances to beat the world champions but we failed," he said. "There were lots of things that could have been done better if I look back to the game. I feel really sad for the loss."

Yao had not been a force in the first two games, scoring just 13 and 11 points. That changed in the third game, against Angola. Yao dominated on both ends of the court, scoring 30 points and blocking four shots. He missed only one field goal attempt, and China never trailed in the game. Yao's performance gave China its first win, 85–68.

The win kept alive China's hopes of reaching the medal round. Those hopes were slim, however. They needed a victory over a powerful German team to advance. Germany was loaded with NBA talent, led by forward Dirk Nowitzki. Most experts expected Germany to easily handle the Chinese.

But China was up to the challenge. Yao came out excited and scored the game's first two baskets. He was doing everything he could to pump up his teammates and the crowd. China kept pouring it on, dominating the first three quarters. Their defense smothered the German shooters. With less than 7 minutes to play, they held a 54–41 lead. But Germany wasn't done. Led by Nowitzki, the Germans outscored China 14–2 over the next several minutes to pull within 2 points.

China led 58–55 with 28 seconds to go after Yi Jianlian knocked down a 15-foot jump shot. The fans in the arena were going wild. Germany had the ball, looking to tie the game. But a Nowitzki 3-pointer missed. Yao gobbled up the rebound and was immediately fouled. He made one of two free throws—his 25th point of the night—and China held on for a shocking 59–55 victory. They were headed to the medal round!

Once again, the first elimination round was as far as the Chinese team would get. Yao and his teammates kept pace at the start of a game against Lithuania. But the powerful Lithuanians soon took control, using a physical style to rough up Yao. They often devoted two or even three defenders to hanging on him and denying him the ball.

With about four minutes to go and the game out of hand, Yao finally left the court, having scored 19 points. He threw his towel down in frustration before sitting with his head in his hands. With the 96–68 defeat, the Chinese team's Olympics were over.

The United States defeated Spain to win the 2008 Olympic gold medal.

"I think we got this far with our courage but we had our limitations," Yao said of the loss. "Of course we are disappointed but we have no regrets."

For Yao, it was time to start thinking about the next season with the Rockets.

Epilogue

Global Superstar

China has more than a billion people, more than one-fifth of the world's total population. Internationally, none of them is more famous or more recognizable than Yao Ming. For decades, China was a nation of isolation. Few outside the country knew the names or faces of its greatest athletes. But Yao has helped to change all of that. His amazing raw ability, his dedication, his sense of humor, and his likable, easygoing personality have made him a hit in China, the United States, and just about everywhere else in the world where basketball is played.

Yao's career numbers don't yet place him among the game's all-time greats. While he has shown flashes of being one of the game's best players, a string of injuries has held him back. After spending three healthy NBA seasons at the beginning of his career, he suffered through three straight seasons that were shortened by injury. He hadn't played in more than 57 regular-season games since 2004–2005, which was a major concern to Rockets fans heading into the 2008–2009 season.

Followers of the team were concerned that Yao may have pushed himself too hard to be ready for the 2008 Olympics. They wondered whether his speedy return to practice after his injury would jeopardize his long-term health. On the other hand, Rockets fans had plenty of reasons to be hopeful about their team's chances. In the off-season, the team had acquired forward Ron Artest from the Sacramento Kings. Artest, known as a defensive specialist, would give the Rockets an added dimension, especially in the playoffs, where defense is important.

Yao, however, was concerned about the addition. Artest, while a great player, was also known for his questionable behavior both on and off the court. Yao expressed his concerns to the media, which caused a small controversy.

Artest seemed unbothered by Yao's doubts. "Once Yao Ming gets to know me, he'll understand what I'm about," Artest assured. And sure enough, Yao quickly got over his concerns.

As the 2008–2009 season opened, all eyes were on Yao and his health. But Yao showed no ill effects from his hurried rehab. He was back in dominant form through the first months of the season, leading the Rockets to a 21–12 record through the end of December. Heading into 2009, the Rockets were in the thick of the Western Conference playoff race. Yao was averaging over 20 points per game and was all but assured of another All-Star Game selection. The season, however, would ultimately be judged on Houston's ability to make the playoffs and then finally advance. Would the addition of Artest be enough of a boost to propel the Rockets to a playoff series victory? This is just one question of many.

What will the long-term future hold for Yao? Will he be able to stay healthy and put up the kind of numbers that could earn him an MVP award or All-NBA First Team honors? He's certainly capable. It's just a matter of whether his body will hold up to the punishing style of the NBA.

And for Yao, team success would be even greater than individual honors. Can he finally lead his team to a playoff series win and perhaps even a trip to the NBA finals? He won a championship in China. Can he manage the same feat in the United States?

We can only guess what the future holds for Yao. But one thing is certain: even if he never plays another NBA game, his legacy will be secure. By coming to the United States and flourishing, he has changed professional basketball forever. He wasn't the first Chinese player to come, but he was the first to

PERSONAL STATISTICS

Name:

Yao Ming

Born:

September 12, 1980

Birthplace:

Shanghai, China

Height:

7' 6"

Weight:

310 lbs.

Position:

Center

CAREER STATISTICS

CBA

Year	Team	Games	RPG	APG	FG%	FT%	PPG
1997–98	Shanghai	21	8.3	1.3	.615	.485	10.0
1998–99	Shanghai	12	12.9	1.7	.585	.699	20.9
1999–00	Shanghai	33	14.5	1.7	.585	.683	21.2
2000–01	Shanghai	22	19.4	2.2	.679	.799	27.1
2001–02	Shanghai	24	19.0	1.9	.721	.759	32.4
Career		112	15.4	1.8	.651	.723	23.4

NBA

Year	Team	Games	RPG	APG	BPG	FG%	FT%	PPG
2002–03	Houston	82	8.2	1.7	1.8	.498	.811	13.5
2003–04	Houston	82	9.0	1.5	1.9	.522	.809	17.5
2004–05	Houston	80	8.4	0.8	2.0	.552	.783	18.3
2005–06	Houston	57	10.2	1.5	1.6	.519	.853	22.3
2006–07	Houston	48	9.4	2.0	2.0	.516	.862	25.0
2007–08	Houston	55	10.8	2.3	2.0	.507	.850	22.0
Career		404	9.2	1.6	1.8	.529	.826	19.0

Abbreviations: RPG, rebounds per game; APG, assists per game; BPG, blocks per game; FG%, field goal percentage; FT%, free-throw percentage; PPG, points per game.

GLOSSARY

draft: a system for selecting new players for professional sports teams

layup: a short, relatively easy shot in which a player lays the ball gently through the basket

field goal: any shot other than a free throw. Depending on where it's taken, a field goal can be worth 2 or 3 points.

osteomyelitis: an infection of the bone or bone marrow

paint: the painted area directly in front of and under the basket. Centers such as Yao typically spend most of their time in or near the paint.

rebound: to collect the ball after a missed shot

rookie: a first-year player

SARS: severe acute respiratory syndrome; a deadly respiratory disease that killed hundreds during an outbreak in China in 2002 and 2003

tibia: a large leg bone that connects the knee to the ankle

turnover: a play in which an offensive player loses control of the ball, giving possession to the other team

SOURCES

3   Brook Larmer, *Operation Yao Ming: The Chinese Sports Empire, American Big Business, and the Making of an NBA Superstar* (New York: Gotham Books, 2005), 277.

6   Yao Ming and Ric Bucher, *Yao: A Life in Two Worlds* (New York: Miramax Books, 2004), 25.

7   C. F. Xiao and Philip Robyn, *Yao Ming: The Road to the NBA* (San Francisco: Long River Press, 2004), 13.

7   Ibid., 28.

8   Ibid., 50.

10   Ibid., 64.

11–12   Ibid., 119.

12   Larmer, *Operation Yao Ming*, 149.

12   Xiao, *The Road to the MBA*, 92.

15   Ibid., 137.

16   Ibid., 144.

17–18   Ibid., 152.

20   Xiao, *The Road to the NBA*, 161.

22   Yao, *Yao: A Life in Two Worlds*, 75.

23   Ibid., 75.

25   Yao, *Yao: A Life in Two Worlds*, 84.

27–28   Xiao, *The Road to the NBA*, 221.

28   Ibid., 222.

30   Ibid., 24.

31   Yao, *Yao: A Life in Two Worlds*, 129.

33   Douglas Choi, The Tao of Yao: Wit and Wisdom from the "Moving Great Wall" Yao Ming (Seattle: Almond Tree Books, 2003), 21.

35   Associated Press, "Yao's Monster Game Can't Derail Mavs," ESPN.com, November 21, 2002, http://sports.espn.go.com/nba/recap?gameId=221121006.

37   Yao, Yao: A Life in Two Worlds, 150.

41   Larmer, *Operation Yao Ming*, 313.

42   Yao, *Yao: A Life in Two Worlds*, 285.

43   Associated Press, "Rockets 123, Hawks 121, 3 OT," *Yahoo Sports*, February 23, 2004, http://sports.yahoo.com/nba/recap?gid=2004022210.

44   Ibid.

47   Associated Press, "Lakers Get Spurs in Next Round," ESPN.com, April 28, 2004, http://sports.espn.go.com/nba/recap?gameId=240428013.

49   John Denton, "McGrady-Francis Swap Official, Finally," *USA Today*, June 29, 2004, http://www.usatoday.com/sports/basketball/nba/2004-06-29-mcgrady-francis-deal_x.htm.

49   "Yao Ming to Bear Chinese Flag at Opening Ceremony," *People's Daily Online*, August 10, 2004, http://english.people.com.cn/200408/09/eng20040809_152347.html.

50   "Bigger, Tougher Squad Carries China's Hoop Hopes," *People's Daily*, August 4, 2004, http://english.hanban.edu.cn/english/sports/102924.htm.

50   Ibid.

51   "Ginóbili's Last-Second Shot Lifts Argentina," *New York Times*, August 16, 2004, http://query.nytimes.com/gst/fullpage?res=9907E1DF133FF935A2575BC0A9629C8B63.

52   Associated Press, "Chinese Overjoyed with Late Win, Knocking out Serbia-Montenegro," SI.com, August 23, 2004, http://sportsillustrated.cnn.com/2004/olympics/2004/basketball/08/23/china.ap/index.html.

52   "Yao: No Shaving for 6 Months if China Misses Final 8," *China Daily*, http://english.hanban.edu.cn/english/sports/103984.htm.

54   "Tops in Toronto," Club Yao News, December 24, 2004, http://www.yaomingmania.com/blog/category/yaos-journal.

56   Associated Press, "NBA Roundup," *New York Times*, April 27, 2005, http://www.nytimes.com/2005/04/27/sports/basketball/27nba.html.

56 Joel Anderson, "NBA: Yao Part of Dynamic Duo," *International Herald Tribune*, April 28, 2005, http://www.iht.com/articles/2005/04/27/sports/yao.php.

56 Anderson, "NBA: Yao Part of Dynamic Duo."

57 Liz Robbins, "Rockets Have Lost Their Grip on Series," *New York Times*, May 1, 2005, http://www.nytimes.com/2005/05/01/sports/basketball/01rockets.html.

57 Ibid.

58 Associated Press, "Mavericks Stall Rockets in Game 7, Cruise to 116–76 Rout," *USA Today*, May 7, 2005, http://www.usatoday.com/sports/basketball/games/2005-05-07-mavericks-rockets-game7_x.htm.

58 Liz Robbins, "NBA: Coach Fined over Yao," *International Herald Tribune*, May 4, 2005, http://www.iht.com/articles/2005/05/03/sports/nba.php.

60 NBA, "Houston Rockets Sign Yao Ming to Multi-year Contract Extension," NBA.com, n.d., http://www.nba.com/rockets/news/Houston_Rockets_Sign_Yao_Ming_-150162-822.html.

60–61 Ibid.

61 NBA, "Houston Rockets Sign Yao Ming to Multi-year Contract Extension."

61 Associated Press, "Grizzlies 86, Rockets 81," Yahoo Sports, November 26, 2005, http://sports.yahoo.com/nba/recap?gid=2005112529.

62 Associated Press, "Rockets 86, Bucks 84," Yahoo Sports, February 2, 2006, http://sports.yahoo.com/nba/recap?gid=2006020110.

63 Chris Duncan, "Rockets 103, Pacers 99," Yahoo Sports, March 9, 2006, http://sports.yahoo.com/nba/recap?gid=2006030810.

63 Chris Duncan, "Rockets 103, Pacers 99," Yahoo Sports, March 9, 2006, http://sports.yahoo.com/nba/recap?gid=2006030810.

64 Doug Alden, "Jazz 85, Rockets 83," Yahoo Sports, April 11, 2006, http://sports.yahoo.com/nba/recap?gid=2006041026.

65 David Barboza, "Waiter, There's a Celebrity in My Shark Fin Soup," *New York Times*, August 13, 2006, http://www.nytimes.com/2006/08/13/weekinreview/13barboza.html.

65 Brian Mahoney, "U.S. Rolls Over Yao Ming, China 121–90," *San Francisco Chronicle*, August 20, 2006, http://www.sfgate.com/cgi-bin/article.cgi?f=/n/a/2006/08/20/sports/s055540D17.DTL.

67 Fran Blinebury, "China Finds Its Own Clutch City to Advance," *Houston Chronicle*, August 24, 2006, http://www.chron.com/disp/story.mpl/sports/bk/bkn/4140378.html.

68 Fran Blinebury, "Yao, China Ousted by Greece at World Basketball Championship," *Houston Chronicle*, August 27, 2006, http://www.chron.com/disp/story.mpl/sports/4144101.html.

66 Mahoney, "U.S. Rolls Over Yao Ming."

69 Jonathan Feigen, "All Rockets Need Is for Talent to Jell," *Houston Chronicle*, October 4, 2006. http://www.chron.com/disp/story.mpl/sports/4234607.html.

69 Ibid.

70 Chris Duncan, "Rockets 107, Mavericks 76," Yahoo Sports, November 5, 2006, http://sports.yahoo.com/nba/recap?gid=2006110410.

70 Liz Robbins, "Yao, Having Best Year, Still Looks to Improve," *New York Times*, November 21, 2006, http://www.nytimes.com/2006/11/21/sports/basketball/21rockets.html?_r=1&oref=slogin.

71 Associated Press, "Rockets 94, Heat 72," Yahoo Sports, November 13, 2006, http://sports.yahoo.com/nba/recap?gid=2006111214.

72 Ivan Carter, "Wizards are Stuck in

the Middle," *Washington Post*, December 10, 2006, http://www.washingtonpost.com/wp-dyn/content/article/2006/12/09/AR2006120901014.html.

73 Jonathan Feigen, "Rockets Lose to Clippers after Yao Breaks Leg," *Houston Chronicle*, December 23, 2006, http://www.chron.com/disp/story.mpl/sports/4423695.html.

73 Ibid.

73 Feigen, "Rockets Lose to Clippers."

74 Matt Becker, "Houston (36–23) at Cleveland (34–25)," Yahoo Sports, March 5, 2007, http://sports.yahoo.com/nba/preview;_ylt=AvITEjD8B1_HbYVEuRF6QeSLvLYF?gid=2007030505&prov=ap.

74–75 Joe Milicia, "Cavaliers 91, Rockets 85," Yahoo Sports, March 5, 2007, http://sports.yahoo.com/nba/recap?gid=2007030505.

75 Associated Press, "Rockets 103, Magic 92," Yahoo Sports, March 11, 2007, http://sports.yahoo.com/nba/recap?gid=2007031110.

77 Duncan, "Utah at Houston."

77 Doug Alden, "Houston at Utah," Yahoo Sports, April 25, 2007, http://sports.yahoo.com/nba/preview?gid=2007042626.

80 Chris Duncan, "Utah at Houston," Yahoo Sports, May 5, 2007, http://sports.yahoo.com/nba/preview?gid=2007050510.

80–81 Michael Murphy, "Yao: Blame Me for First-Round Flameout," *Houston Chronicle*, May 6, 2007, http://www.chron.com/disp/story.mpl/sports/bk/bkn/4779281.html.

85 Brett Martel, "Yao Ming, Tracy McGrady Lead Rockets Past Hornets for 11th-Straight Win," Yahoo Sports, February 22, 2008, http://sports.yahoo.com/nba/recap;_ylt=AkvhmEfs_54sXRiOMA9sgreLvLYF?gid=2008022203&prov=ap.

86 Associated Press, "Yao Done for the Season with Stress Fracture in Left Foot," ESPN.com, February 27, 2008, http://sports.espn.go.com/nba/news/story?id=3265631.

86 Ibid.

88 "Yao Ming Tells Fans He is Targeting Olympic Return," *China Daily*, March 7, 2008, http://www.chinadaily.com.cn/sports/2008-03/07/content_6518379.htm.

89 Harvey Araton, "Injured and Defeated, Yao Treasures the Moment," *New York Times*, August 10, 2008, http://www.nytimes.com/2008/08/11/sports/olympics/11araton.html.

89 Ibid.

90 Xinhua News Agency, "Spain Clinches 85–75 Overtime Win over China," China.org.cn, August 12, 2008, http://www.china.org.cn/olympic/2008-08/12/content_16203182.htm.

92 Reuters, "Jasikevicius Scores 23 to Lead Lithuania Past China," ESPN.com, August 20, 2008, http://sports.espn.go.com/oly/summer08/basketball/men/recap?gameId=817.

94 "Report: Artest Replies to Yao, Seeks 'Commitment' from Rockets," *ESPN.com*, July 31, 2008, http://sports.espn.go.com/nba/news/story?id=3512419.

BIBLIOGRAPHY

Choi, Douglas. *The Tao of Yao: Wit and Wisdom from the Moving Great Wall Yao Ming.* Seattle: Almond Tree Books, 2003.

Larmer, Brook. *Operation Yao Ming: The Chinese Sports Empire, American Big Business, and the Making of an NBA Superstar.* New York: Gotham Books, 2005.

Xiao, C. F. *Yao Ming: The Road to the NBA.* San Francisco: Long River Press, 2004.

Yao Ming and Ric Bucher. *Yao: A Life in Two Worlds.* New York: Miramax Books, 2004.

WEBSITES

Basketball-Reference.com

http://www.basketball-reference.com

Basketball Reference is packed with NBA statistics. Type Yao's name into the search box to get almost any statistic imaginable on the star center.

Club Yao

http://www.yaomingfanclub.com

The official Yao Ming fan club site is loaded with information on the Chinese star. It includes news archives, photos, and even the occasional journal entry from Yao himself.

NBA.com

http://www.nba.com

The official site of the NBA has all the latest news, scores, standings, and statistics.

INDEX

105